Companions in the Between

Companions in the Between

Augustine, Desmond, and
Their Communities of Love

Renée Köhler-Ryan

With a Foreword by
William Desmond

James Clarke & Co

James Clarke & Co

P.O. Box 60
Cambridge
CB1 2NT
United Kingdom

www.jamesclarke.co
publishing@jamesclarke.co

Paperback ISBN: 978 0 227 17750 1
PDF ISBN: 978 0 227 90749 8

British Library Cataloguing in Publication Data
A record is available from the British Library

First Published by Pickwick Publications, 2019

This edition published by James Clarke & Co, 2021
by arrangement with Wipf and Stock Publishers

Copyright © Renée Köhler-Ryan, 2019

All rights reserved. No part of this edition may be reproduced, stored electronically or in any retrieval system, or transmitted in any form or by any means, electronic, mechanical, photocopying, recording, or otherwise, without prior written permission from the Publisher (permissions@jamesclarke.co).

For Berenice Fenn (1919–2018),
who married Alvin in the church of St. Augustine, Tucson, Arizona

I admit that I find it easy to abandon my whole self to the love of [my closest and most intimate friends], especially when I am wearied by the scandals of the world, and I find rest in that love without any worry. I, of course, feel that God is in that person to whom I abandon myself with security and in whom I find rest in security. And in that security I do not at all fear that incertitude of tomorrow stemming from . . . human fragility . . . For, when I perceive that a man is aflame with Christian love and has become my loyal friend with that love, whatever of my plans and thoughts I entrust to him I do not entrust to a human being, but to him in whom he remains so that he is such a person.

SAINT AUGUSTINE, *LETTER 73.10* (TO SAINT JEROME)

Table of Contents

Foreword by William Desmond ix
Introduction xv

PART 1: *Creation and Reflection: Augustine, Desmond, and Cosmos*

Chapter 1: An Archaeological Ethics:
   Augustine, Desmond, and Digging Back to the Agapeic Origin 3
Chapter 2: "No Block Creation": Good and Evil in
   William Desmond's Augustinian Philosophy of Elemental Order 19

PART 2: *Becoming Porous: The Aesthetics of Prayerful Contemplation*

Chapter 3: Gifted Beggars in the *Metaxu*: A Study of the Platonic and
   Augustinian Resonances of Porosity in *God and the Between* 35
Chapter 4: Thinking Transcendence, Transgressing the Mask:
   Desmond Pondering Augustine and Thomas Aquinas 60
Chapter 5: On Speaking the Amen:
   Augustinian Soliloquy and Shakespearean Porosity in the *Metaxu* 82

PART 3: *Citizenship in the Between: Building the Porous City*

Chapter 6: Love and Friendship in the *Metaxu*:
   Becoming Agapeic in Community 101
Chapter 7: Intimate Friendship and the Christian Cosmopolis:
   Jerome's Challenge in the *Metaxu* 119

Bibliography 145
Index 153

Foreword

I AM VERY PLEASED to offer a foreword to a work like this. It is a work which takes as central the notion of companioning in my own writings, and in the relation of these to other thinkers of note, and perhaps St. Augustine of most note. Renée Köhler-Ryan's book is a work on companioning, yet it is a work that itself is companioning. Indeed I take the practice of her thinking to exemplify something of what being a companion in thought might entail. I have long admired the sapiential genuineness of her writings over the years and am delighted to see these writings gathered here together, extended sometimes from earlier versions, and deftly molded into an admirable work of philosophical and theological reflection. It is a work in which also there is wise porosity among the aesthetic, the ethical, and the religious.

While Renée lucidly outlines what companioning might entail, perhaps it might be helpful to add a word on what companioning is. I have often been asked about the relation of my efforts at philosophical thought to theological concerns. The question is also sometimes posed as to whether philosophy and theology need each other. I find the question pressing because modern philosophy on the whole has a tendency to define itself primarily as autonomous, as marked by thought that claims to be essentially self-determining. The result is hard to avoid: philosophy will tend to deny any need of theology, even to the point of its rebuffing any approach by theology. This point, of course, has implications for philosophy's relation to its others in a wider sense. What of its relation to art, for instance, and indeed to science? Why is religion, and mediately theology, singled out for special rebuff? Why should art or science get treated differently, treated more tenderly? If philosophy demands to be self-determining, its character tends not to be receptive, in the first instance, to what is other to itself. And not receptive in the last instance also, given that if the significant other is to approach philosophy, it will only be accepted on the terms determined by philosophy itself, and hence the approach will not be quite the drawing near of the other as truly other.

But suppose philosophy, as I think, is *metaxological*, that is, to be essentially defined by its offering a *logos* of the *metaxu*, what then? The practice of philosophy is inseparable from its relation to its significant others. Throughout the long history of different practices of philosophy, our being religious, and mediately, our being theological, have been the most significant of philosophy's other. Self-determining philosophy is not metaxological in this regard: there is to be nothing between it and theology, for it would define itself as for itself. To ask again if philosophy and theology need each other, one would have to say "yes" in a certain sense. The "yes" would also include openness to other significant others, the artistic or poetic, for instance. How then do philosophy and its others retain any freedom? Do they retain their respective freedoms? Ingredient in the answer must be a more plurivocal understanding of freedom that does not delimit freedom univocally to autonomous self-determination. Being in relation to what is other to self-determination forms part of what is at issue in such a plurivocal understanding of freedom. And we might ask: Is there is a kind of "heteronomy" involved in being in metaxological relation, a heteronomy not only generous to the other but in receipt of the generosity of the other?

It is here that one can see the significance of the companioning approach. The companion is an other who, at best, is generously there in the between to offer endowments of presence and support and aid, and indeed often secret gifts of elemental presence. The offer of such gifts witnesses a being-there that is the being-with of love. Do philosophy and theology need each other? In light of what I have just said, we are enabled to think of companions whose "need" of each other is not constraining but *releasing*. Such a sense of companioning is central to this work of Renée Köhler-Ryan.

Such a releasing need is not a dyadic relation in which each might engage the other but not enter intimately into the life of the other. Nor is it simply dialectical, if we define this in the modern way as philosophy including the theological in its own self-determining thinking. Again, I would say the need is metaxological, in that our being both religious and philosophical are intimate others in a porous between where what is most original and ultimate is to be diversely engaged. If philosophy and theology do need each other, the need is such a companioning one. Companions can be themselves, and yet if they are bound together, they may need each other but not always out of need alone. If companions break bread together, it is their shared need of what is beyond them both that binds them. Renée's work is admirably attuned to the promise of such companionship, and not only as a matter of reflection but more importantly as a matter of participation. Her book gives true witness to participation in this companioning.

The issue here is not on boundary questions between philosophy and theology in an academic sense but on their porosity to each other in a living sense. Our being is to be religious, and this is to be understood in an ontological rather than academic sense. Being philosophical and theological each can refer to an exigence of thought marking our condition of being between, or each can be seen as more formal academic disciplines. This book takes the exigence as more primordial than the discipline, while showing that the exigence points to the discipline to be understood in a fuller sense. Augustine especially as a companion can communicate to us the living exigence, as well as the sense that the discipline without the exigence can become an intellectual *technē* without animating soul.

While I myself have wanted to engage with Augustine in this companioning sense, and not simply as a scholar in a technical, professional sense, Renée engages both myself and Augustine in the same spirit. And not only Augustine, of course. She does exemplary justice to the way I have counted Augustine as a companion in my own efforts to think about fundamental questions, such as God and the soul, the nature of desire and love, and one's being in community with the neighbor. But there are others like Plato or Aquinas or Shakespeare to whom one relates not as objects of research but as companioning one's own search. The other thinker or writer is a source of inspiration and challenge, not always explicitly acknowledged as such, but of influence perhaps at a more intimate level, providing something like a secret touchstone, in relation to intellectual and spiritual excellence. Of course, in conversation with a companion one might be tempted to project one's own thoughts onto the other and take one's own thoughts as if they were that of the companion. I call this the ventriloquizing approach. One uses the other to make that other say the things that one would want to say in any case, regardless of what the other actually says. This is always a temptation but true companions manage to transcend ventriloquizing and learn to listen. Of course, one need not always agree with the companion, even as the companion may reprimand and correct one. The communicative passage between oneself and others, others and oneself, is the life of wording the between in fidelity to all of us being true.

Diverse dimensions of that companioning approach are shown in the present work. In the metaxological orientation what counts is less the erection of formal boundaries between disciplines as the ability to *pass between* philosophy and theology, beyond dyadic exclusion and dialectical inclusion, and without dodging hard questions in an equivocal middling fudge. The companioning side of the present work reveals rich possibilities of conversation in friendship, richer than in *polemos*, richer than in *agon*. Seek the truth with love: the work gives new freshness to philosophy understood as sapiential. This is something old, and something always to be renewed. The deepest point about companioning is not struggle, not competition, but mindfully being with the other in the embrace of a superior call on us to be truthful in the company of truth.

Needless to say, something of the more personal voice inevitably is to be heard in this sapiential orientation. One might echo Pierre Hadot: philosophy of old was a way of life, not just a theory or the construction of a system. The personal voice resounds in Renée's work. To take one instance: I found very illuminating the way her reflection on person as mask, and on mask as *personans*, threw significant light on the company of my own thought with that of Augustine and Aquinas. What comes across is the figure of the thinker as a place of passage and communication, porous to the divine at depths of intimacy the thinker herself or himself mostly does not know explicitly at all. Often the significance is revealed, or perhaps suggested, at certain extremities, such as Aquinas's retraction into sacred silence. I think also of the striking extremity of Macbeth's not being able to say "Amen," so well explored here in connection with Shakespeare's play. In the silence of one, the word has come, making further human words straw; in the other, the word does not come at all, and the "Amen" sticks in the throat.

Renée is very deft in lighting on illuminating possibilities in my own work and bringing it into conversation with other companions. The between space is articulated as multiply traversed, and this not only by thinkers but also in relation to central themes in ethics, aesthetics, religion, and metaphysics. In addition to the surprising connections with respect to the mask and the "Amen," as well as her bringing together of Macbeth and Augustine in relation to the soliloquy, I am intrigued at her sensitivity to my relation to Aquinas. She discerns the point about the forensic univocity of the surface, and the need of the reader of Aquinas to be a listener beyond the univocities of the rational surface. Among other things, I am taken by her archaeological exploration of the original good of the "to be," by connections made between the elemental and creation, by her sensitivities to the relation of prayer and porosity, by her sense of thinking itself as endowed, by her discerning feeling for the mixing of the Cities of Man and God in our sojourn in time, and the challenge to us to read wisely the often perplexing signs of agapeic community. I also find a feel for the surprise of revelation, being put in mind of the disciples at Emmaus who were gifted with a second awakening though they seemed already to be awake, a second awakening that was an awakening for the first time. Metaxology here asks for *metanoia*. Companioning thought can seed a metanoetics. The gifted eyes of love truly see what is lovely—and see the lovely because it is lovely.

It is a pleasure to hear the voice of Renée but in that also to find something of oneself again in Renée's voice. I do not mean the pleasure of vanity but more the finding of one's own voice othered through the voice of a discerning other; and in this, coming back to oneself newly, like and unlike, that is, newly in a renewing way. I take this to be the mark of the conversation of companions. Releasing companionship is also refreshing of the companions. The companion is not a simple mirror that reflects an original back to itself point by point. Passage in the between with nuance of communication transforms the plurivocal intimacy of communication. There is a passage between companions that augments the between in giving itself to the other, and that augments itself in giving itself over to the other and giving itself away. The response of the other brings one out of oneself. But it more than just allows one to be seen newly or differently; it releases one to see things anew—old things and things now becoming new to one, becoming newly friendly, becoming new friends. In companioning one learns as much about the others as about one's own otherness. Renée's voice speaks for itself intelligently, engagingly, lucidly, communicatively, and wisely. It is a privilege to have a companion such as Renée in whose company we come to know that we are lifted up. To be gifted with such companions is to be graced. This is a gracious work for whose gift one is grateful.

William Desmond
David Cook Chair of Philosophy, Villanova University, USA
Thomas A. F. Kelly Visiting Chair in Philosophy,
    Maynooth University, Ireland
Professor of Philosophy Emeritus, Institute of Philosophy,
    KU Leuven, Belgium

Introduction

COMPANIONSHIP IS AT THE heart of philosophical work that strives to discover the truth of what it means to be human. Companions break and consume bread together, and in this communally enjoyed nourishment, they can participate in fulfilled desires for intimacy with others. That intimacy brings with it a greater knowledge of the self, and more importantly of how the self is constantly thrown beyond itself, related to that which lies beyond. For Augustine, such self-understanding only happens when in communication with God—that limitless mystery of love at the root of all our desires and relationships. Philosophers and theologians—and poets and artists too—form a community that spans millennia, of persons earnestly attuned to finding and expressing the meaning of existence. These responses to being—to the "passion of being" that William Desmond refers to in the title of one of his more recent works[1]—appreciate that communities of inquiry are possible only because of a divinely bestowed gift. To paraphrase a scriptural verse, we are called to know and love the world, because through that world the divine has first made something of itself known, through the love that humans experience in various manifestations.[2]

Humans have the capacity to wonder, and thus to be *porous*[3] to the way that creation moves in and through us, as we respond to its manifestations of divine mystery. Any contemporary thinker can look back to a predecessor, and find in him or her an approach to being and to the divine mystery that resonates and inspires. William Desmond argues that such an earlier explorer can become a companion in thought. The fourth chapter of this volume discusses how Desmond thinks of both Augustine and Thomas Aquinas as such companions. Here it is worthwhile to signal further the

1. Desmond, *Gift of Beauty*.
2. 1 John 4:19.
3. This term runs throughout Desmond's work and will be discussed throughout this volume.

significance of Augustine and Desmond's relationship in thought as that of companions, thereby discussing the significance of the title and major themes of this book.

Desmond has written of what he calls a "companioning approach" that a thinker can take, whereby

> a particular thinker is a source of inspiration and challenge, not always explicitly acknowledged as such, but of influence perhaps at a more intimate level, providing something like a secret touchstone, in relation to intellectual and spiritual excellence.[4]

He identifies Augustine in particular as such a companion, and the present work traces out some of the ways in which that companionship has impressed its intimate delineations within Desmond's metaxological philosophy.[5] His significant gift to possible present and future companions is his metaxological approach to metaphysics, which simultaneously opens up pathways between various modes of thought, by delving into the ways that humans find themselves in the world and at the same time thrown beyond it. The thinker of the *metaxu* is alert to the hyperbolic modes of thought, finding whispers of divine intimacy in the dimensions of human life. This opens up possibilities for philosophers to engage in multifarious ways with other disciplines. Where the modern and contemporary tendency in philosophy has been to segregate areas of inquiry, Desmond's thought makes the case that each is porous to the others. As a philosopher he can speak to theologians, artists, poets, ethicists, and political scientists—and thereby find more possibilities for companionship. Similarly, Augustine has much to say not only to his fellow theologians and pastors, but also to philosophers, and those who seek truth, beauty, and goodness in all its forms. Both Augustine and Desmond appreciate that when philosophy and theology are porous to one another, findings are both rich and immense.

In Desmond's work, one can discern Augustinian ways of questioning—prayerful, perplexed, passionate, and personally engaged.[6] Even when not developing a specifically Augustinian question or concept, Desmond's manner of philosophizing follows what he identifies as the Augustinian

---

4. Desmond, "Superiority Beyond Interiority."

5. Metaxological philosophy considers being in its various dimensions as "between." This is discussed throughout this book, and in particular in chapter 3. It is also discussed further below in this introduction.

6. Arguably, one sees this in particular in *God and the Between*, where Desmond's Cantos set a prayerful space for philosophy.

pathway—from exterior to interior, from inferior to superior. Thereby, Augustine's recognition that we are never alone but constantly in relation to God, self, others, and the cosmos, permeates metaxological considerations. Desmond also occasionally recalls Augustine's claim in the *Soliloquies* that all he wants to know are God and the soul—"nothing more." Both God and soul are infinite sources for inquiry. Augustine knows that he will need help to get anywhere at all in exploring these. This will be aid from God, but also from those who have provoked him to think, in various communities. Thus, Augustine relies on Monica and Alypius, Cicero and Plato, Ambrose, those whom he serves as a pastor and bishop, and those with whom he carries out correspondence. At the same time, he is in conversation with those before him who have transmitted the Word of God through Church and history. In the company of others, Augustine can carry out his inquiries; and he can see more than he could have if working alone. Like Augustine, Desmond acknowledges those with whom he looks ahead. While both Augustine and Desmond gaze in the same direction, Desmond explicitly and implicitly develops Augustine's perspective on that vista. The following chapters develop another standpoint, which is that Augustine can be viewed through a metaxological lens. Thereby, taking a companioning approach both with and between Augustine and Desmond, we can see further, but also in more depth and detail, what it means to think and pray in the *between*.

Metaxological philosophy studies the *metaxu*, which Desmond translates as the *between* or the *middle*. Desmond takes the term from Plato's *Symposium*, where it refers to *eros*. The one who embarks on metaxological philosophy is driven by fruitful restlessness that characterizes all of Augustine's work. Such inquiry can only find rest in God, which is to say in *agape*, or *caritas*; however, such rest is by no means stationary. Human existence is lived between various forces, or potencies, each of which influences all the others. Metaxological inquiry seeks to explore and express what it means to be in the middle; but also how metaphysics is *per se* metaxological. That is, if being is characterized by the porosity that humans find in their everyday lives, how can philosophers—or indeed, any thinkers—articulate this?

One way to answer this question is to compare the metaxological with other ways of thinking that Desmond develops, discusses, and incorporates. He speaks of the univocal, equivocal, and dialectical approaches to being; each of these is important, but insufficient for disclosing the fullness of being. According to the univocal, thinkers strive to find and develop how being speaks in one way, or one voice. If this were our only means to approach reality, we would be forced eventually into silence. As it is, the univocal is only one way of being and being known, important to metaxological philosophy not least because it explains the sense of oneness that humans can experience *with* being. Such unification grounds what Desmond calls the *idiocy of being*, which is a felt elemental oneness that cannot quite be put into words, but which nonetheless strives to say how it feels to be. Negatively, the univocal can be subverted to say that being only speaks in one way; nothing else becomes permissible, and the result is tyranny for thought and action.

Equivocity brings us to another way in which being speaks so that we can articulate it. While the univocal stresses sameness, equivocity pertains to difference that cannot be pinned down by one (univocal) way of saying what is. Positively, equivocity draws our attention to the plurality of being—its plurivocity; it underscores that being cannot be restrained, because it is always changing, constantly becoming. Being is always in surplus; it is beyond the possibility of complete mediation. Without another mode of enquiry to supplement its discoveries, the equivocal can tear thought from being—making it seem as though meaning is an illusion and nothing can be known.

Dialectic enters as a third way to philosophize, which mediates the univocal and the equivocal, such that they do not settle into shallow oneness or dissipate into fragmentary plurality. Dialectic in this sense was brought to perfection by Hegel. An expert in Hegel's thought, Desmond draws attention to how deficient such dialectic is when it becomes a closed system rather than an open whole. Dialectic stresses mediation, such that the subject overcomes the other, subsuming other into self so that there is no surplus. All is rationalized, and much is explained away. The problems with dialectic may now be apparent; rather than maintaining the strengths of the univocal and equivocal—letting them speak—the dialectical reduces all to one story, or picture, of being—where everything is a piece of a complete whole, and nothing lies beyond.

Beyond the closed dialectic of Hegel's modernity is the metaxological, which Desmond thinks of as an open dialectic. The metaxological is speech, or discourse, about the middle named by *metaxu*. As such, the metaxological distinguishes *between* all, without thereby obliterating any, of the various ways in which being speaks. The metaxological stresses that there is a community of beings in which all forms of human being-together are grounded. Hence, metaxological philosophy listens to the univocal.

INTRODUCTION

At the same time, it seeks out where differences lie, and accentuates those equivocities. This then makes space for the self-mediating possibilities of dialectic, bringing them to the point of *Aufhebung*, or sublation. That is to say, dialectic goes so far and no further. Finding that point of unmediated surplus brings the metaxological into its own, with implications for metaphysics and at the same time for every way in which we live our lives.

All of these ideas are present in the following chapters, especially for how they can be deepened via resources in one of Desmond's main influences: Augustine. Throughout his work, Desmond is in dialog with various thinkers—philosophers, theologians, poets—and some of these he refers to as companions in thought. In this respect, Augustine is a significant figure for developing metaxological philosophy. That is to say, Desmond identifies Augustine as someone who has influenced his philosophical approaches, by being a companion in thought. The chapters of this book go into specific detail about what such companionship entails. For now, identifying some key themes and points of reference will orientate what follows.

Firstly, the way Augustine contemplates *between* thought and prayer, and also between metaphysics, aesthetics, ethics, and politics, is, to use Desmond's term, a very *metaxological* approach. Augustine is a synthetic thinker. Knowledge is connected and never arbitrary. Ultimately, it indicates the existence of a personal relationship to the divine. Augustine is driven to find the personal implications of what is true. When he discovers such impacts, he makes known his findings, to whichever audience he finds most appropriate. These are aspects that Desmond shares with him. Secondly, Desmond identifies repeatedly the importance of the Augustinian journey, from exterior to interior and inferior to superior. Tracing this pathway through Desmond's thought at key points reveals something more about how we think, pray, and live in communities. A final point for now: there are moments while reading either Augustine or Desmond when thought and prayerful contemplation merge into one another; each shares in a space that Desmond calls a "Sabbath for Thought." Philosophy is porous to religion, so that thinking about *what* is takes us to *Who* is. Thus, both thinkers are significant to developing a key theme in Judaeo-Christian thought: that metaphysics is ultimately a study of relationship to God. As such, it makes ethical and political demands. The beauty of such calling resonates in every human, restless, heart.

The chapters in this book bring together the thoughts of over a decade. Part 1, "Creation and Reflection: Augustine, Desmond, and Cosmos," examines how Augustine's view of creation might further inform Desmond's metaxological appreciation of the cosmos. The first chapter, "An Archaeological Ethics: Augustine, Desmond, and Digging Back to the Agapeic Origin," argues that Augustine's *Confessions* helps to understand how metaphysical investigation of the goodness of being is tied up with the question of how to be good. When we find the origin of the universe, we find ourselves; but this is the beginning rather than the end of our relationship with divine transcendence. This chapter notes that contemplating ourselves in relationship with God through creation means moving away from that tendency in modern philosophical deism, whereby the universe is thought of as a "block creation." Chapter 2 picks up on that point, to develop a very Augustinian answer. Namely, both Augustine and Desmond refuse to consider creation mechanistically, as something made and then abandoned. Instead of thinking it as a block wherein all possibilities are from the moment of creation, fully contained and no longer in need of relationship with God, both thinkers maintain that the cosmos is in dynamic and constant relationship with the Creator. Only then can we make sense of good and evil in the world, in terms of the development of relationship with what is divine, here, and also beyond.

Part 2 turns to themes to do with "Becoming Porous" by exploring "The Aesthetics of Prayerful Contemplation." Chapter 3 begins by discussing the importance of recognizing that to be *porous* to the divine in the cosmos is to see how important it is that we are not self-sufficient. Like *Eros* in the *Symposium*, we are both impoverished and gifted. Considering this, metaxological thinkers can adopt Augustine's sense that to pray is to be both gifted and beggarly. Augustine muses that when we pray, we do not tell God anything he does not already know about us; instead, we actively pursue a relationship with him that depends on expressing just how much we need God for everything. *Agape* thus presents as the source for every form of *erotic* longing and selving. Chapter 4 then discusses the companionship that Desmond claims he has with both Augustine and Thomas Aquinas. At the same time, it develops a theme prevalent in Desmond's thought, of the mask in relationship to doubling. Essentially, "Thinking Transcendence, Transgressing the Mask: Desmond Pondering Augustine and Thomas Aquinas" draws on some of the insights about prayer in the previous chapter. It goes further to link the idea of being a gifted beggar with analogy and surplus. Augustine, Thomas, and Desmond all strive to articulate the overabundance of God, and how one can relate to such richness. Masks become important points of mediation between us and God, so as to dwell in relation to divine resource. Finally, chapter 5 attempts more explicitly to develop what is at stake in the communities that we form in the *metaxu*. Entitled "On Speaking the Amen: Augustinian Soliloquy and Shakespearean Porosity in the *Metaxu*," this chapter examines how Desmond speaks about *Macbeth* as a play that examines the potential dangers of equivocity. At the same time, it brings together Augustine's specific understanding and invention of the term *soliloquy* to argue that Macbeth violates the relationship between self and others. This leads to his incapacity to know either God or self. With metaxological thought at its foundation, this chapter demonstrates, through reading one of Macbeth's soliloquies, that Shakespearean tragedy can be considered an inverted Augustinian journey.

With part 2 ending on a plea for well-ordered forms of community, part 3 develops some ways to think through what such communities entail. Entitled "Citizenship in the Between: Building the Porous City," the final part explores both the implications and the challenges of living out Augustine's ethical and political vision. Chapter 6, "Love and Friendship in the *Metaxu*: Becoming Agapeic in Community," examines the universal agapeic call and the special role of friendship for those in the City of God. Taking issue with the notion that Augustine thinks of the City of Man and the City of God as completely separate, discussion here points toward intermingling between the cities—and thus to the intermediations that are so important to metaxological philosophy. Augustine thinks that all humans are related at a biological level (we are all descended from Adam) and that our kinship is fulfilled in agapeic love. Placing this alongside Desmond's exploration of the various forms of community (especially communities of agapeic service) elucidates some of ethical and political implications of metaxological philosophy. Finally, chapter 7 recognizes the challenges faced by those who strive to live out the promise of agapeic love. It takes up the Augustinian tension whereby Christians are both to love every person as one loves oneself and to have intimate friendships whereby the beloved is another self. This seemingly contradictory demand—to love everyone, and then only a select few, as one loves oneself—is interpreted in light of Desmond's distinction between the cosmopolis and the ghetto, which can be synthesised in what he calls the *intimate universal*. Nonetheless, there are challenges to those striving for the universal while living in communities where *agape* is intimately experienced. The altercation between Augustine and Jerome brings these to light. Their correspondence offers a rare insight into the

Introduction

limitations for *agape* between Christians who disagree with one another, and who can only communicate (due to distance) in the written word. The boundaries and possibilities for what Desmond calls agapeic communities of service thereby come to light. Considering these offers challenges to contemporary scholars who might strive to become companions in thought.

This volume consolidates the work of a decade. It would not exist at all were it not for many companions in thought, at each step of the way. First among these is William Desmond, whose generosity at every point has been essential—from suggesting the book, to providing me with background material and suggestions, to writing the foreword, and most especially for his guidance and friendship over the years. With him I likewise thank Maria Desmond. Various chapters are indebted to editors, conference organizers, and colleagues, particularly as four of the chapters here collected and re-edited have been published previously. Among these I acknowledge in particular Thomas A. F. Kelly (now deceased), Martin Moors, Frederiek Depoortere and Jacques Haers, Gregory Grimes, Christopher Ben Simpson, Brendan Sammon, Dennis Vanden Auweele, John Hymers, Miles Smit, James McGuirk, and Sydney Palmer C'de Baca. I thank my colleagues at the Institute of Philosophy at the Katholieke Universiteit Leuven, and also those at University of Notre Dame Australia, who have made it possible for me to take the sabbatical that meant I could finally complete this project. I also thank librarians at the Katholieke Universiteit Leuven, University of Notre Dame Australia, and at the Veech Library at the Catholic Institute of Sydney. I thank too my parents, siblings, grandparents (in particular my maternal grandmother, Berenice Fenn, who passed away last year), and extended family for all of their love and support. Finally, I thank my husband, Jo, and our children, for their patience and love on this pilgrim journey.

PART 1

*Creation and Reflection:
Augustine, Desmond, and Cosmos*

1

An Archaeological Ethics

Augustine, Desmond, and Digging Back to the Agapeic Origin

THIS CHAPTER SETS INTO motion an Augustinian trajectory of thought, traced through various interconnecting paths in the thought of William Desmond. In particular, it traces some Augustinian resonances within William Desmond's thought, regarding the relation between the metaxological ethos and its agapeic origin. Desmond is perhaps most explicit in his invocation of Augustine in his Introduction to *Desire, Dialectic and Otherness: An Essay on Origins*,[1] a work which he there describes as "an Augustinian odyssey, embarked on in the wake of Hegel." Like Augustine, he says, he wishes "to do justice to the self-knowledge of desire and its openness to otherness, without falling into unacceptable dualism."[2] In effect this means that Desmond wants to steer away from a sense of the origin as static, as set apart both from us and the created order. This has many implications for his thought, which might perhaps come into bolder relief when seen in light of some aspects of Augustine's work. Both thinkers ground their movement in a sense of an origin to be sought throughout the created order, in an erotic striving toward the constantly issuing agapeic giver of being. This trajectory cannot be understood as strictly teleological, but rather as *archaeological*, as a quest for an origin that implicates within itself that *arche* from which the created order comes forth.

---

1. See also Desmond, "Augustine's *Confessions*," which discusses some of the major elements focussed on in the present chapter.
2. Desmond, *Desire*, 13–14.

Such movement cannot, then, be imagined in strictly linear terms. Desmond often quotes Augustine's maxim, *ab exterioribus ad interiora; ab inferioribus ad superior*.[3] His understanding of the self's interiority, in relation both to creation and to the transcendent Creator, is very mindful of these words. Augustine couples this double progression with an advance from restlessness toward peace. "Our heart is unquiet until it rests in you,"[4] he prays. Yet, after his conversion, the saint is not in any kind of stasis. His sense of restlessness indicates the non-finite, unbounded nature of its ground. Before turning to God, his restlessness is characterized by an eroticism without nuance and devoid of real focus. Afterwards it is transformed and directed, but not toward any finite goal. He knows now that his desire is for something other than himself, and yet he is already suffused from within, and simultaneously outwardly surrounded, by divine goodness. His source of peace is the overabundant answer to his inquietude. Here, then, we see two factors also very much at stake in Desmond's Augustinian odyssey. Firstly, our movement is such that our infinite inquietude can only be set to rest in an infinite source of peace, where the transcendent breaks through any naïve sense we might have of God as the finite end of our desires. Secondly, striving towards God does not demand a dualistic vision that precludes appreciation for creation. Instead our focus on the Creator intensifies our love for creatures.

These points are interrelated, because they hearken to the nature of the *agapeic origin*, as Desmond calls it throughout *Being and the Between* and *Ethics and the Between*, or *the absolute original*, as in *Desire, Dialectic and Otherness*. These works all stress the sense that being is good, and that it is good to be. That is, the ethos in which we live is charged with meaning, because the one who has given the gift of being is superabundant, and this excess flows into every one of his creatures. For humans, this additionally means a plenitude in the range of communication with and of the good, directed toward both creation and Creator. This overabundance of possible meanings might be seen as infinite, but such infinitude must be qualified. Thus in *Desire, Dialectic and Otherness*, Desmond distinguishes among three forms of infinitude.[5] The more linear form of *infinite succession* refers

---

3. Desmond quotes this in *Desire*, 13.

4. Augustine, *Confessions*, 1.1: *inquietum est cor nostrum donec requiescat in te*. Rex Warner translates this as "Our hearts are restless until they rest in Thee." Pine-Coffin renders it "Our hearts find no peace until they find rest in you." Boulding translates: "Our heart is unquiet until it rests in you."

5. See in particular Desmond, *Desire*, 149–54.

to the constant becoming and multifariousness of creatures. According to this aspect, nature appears as progressing toward a not completely definable end. We can distinguish lines of similarity, in species of animals for example, but variations in these lines seem to us limitless. Infinite succession can overwhelm us with its equivocity, with its constant emergence into such varied forms. If this were all we knew of infinitude, we would be scattered in our attempts to find meaning in our own infinite restlessness. *Intentional infinitude* changes such a perspective, setting us apart from this endless chain of progression. In Desmond's words, "intentional infinitude specifically refers to the power of open dialectical self-mediation displayed in the articulation of human desire."[6] Human desire seeks unity, rather than dispersal. We want to mediate between ourselves and the world; but more, we want to communicate ourselves to ourselves. Desmond describes this potency as circular, though not in a closed way, and founded in the appreciation that humans seek to know themselves. In this search they strive for open wholeness, as the desired end to their infinite restlessness. As Augustine so well knew, however, no such integrity is possible through introspection alone. We must not only move inward; we must strive upward. This then brings us to *actual infinitude*, whereby we are opened up to "the sense of something more."[7] That is, we become open to an intuitive knowledge of the transcendent, of something that so far exceeds our possibilities of disclosure to ourselves and the world that we are in touch again with the surplus value of being. The transcendent breaks through our consciousness of the immanent, in such a way that our consciousness of the significance of creation is heightened rather than diminished—as it would be according to any dualistic signification. Actual infinitude brings us to the source of every other infinitude. It brings us to our absolute original, our agapeic origin. We are henceforth in a realm of paradox, where language can strive toward the expression of ultimate meaning, and yet must always fail.

Thus Desmond speaks in terms of "the paradoxical coupling of wholeness and openness, completeness and infinity . . . an overwholeness, as it were."[8] Our movement toward this actual infinitude as the open end of our quest is fundamentally Augustinian. Further indication of this is Augustine's appreciation for the need of enigmatic language when speaking of his ultimate source of peace. The *Confessions* in particular take the form of a

---

6. Desmond, *Desire*, 150.
7. Desmond, *Desire*, 151.
8. Desmond, *Desire*, 152.

prayer of praise, keeping the question in mind throughout: How can one pray to you unless he knows you?[9] This desire for prayer becomes one with the desire for knowledge of the Creator, and this coupled desire forms a more profound mindfulness toward the ultimate.

In fact, this movement of our inward desire toward our origin calls for us to become mindful toward both the world in which we live and the actual, infinite transcendence that suffuses this universe with value. These significations are for Desmond best expressed in his elaborations of the metaxological. So, when he asks at the beginning of chapter 5 of *Ethics and the Between*, "Where are we?,"[10] his question is more than rhetorical. It brings us to the core of his metaphysics. We are precisely here, in the between, in the overdetermined matrix of the metaxological, as it reminds us that it is good to be. The univocal and dialectical modes of inquiry, taken separately, cannot bring us to ultimacy. Together, though, they anticipate a richer sense of what it is to be, so that they can be taken up into a full appreciation of the good with which we are at one, and yet which exceeds us. Here in the between, a dualistic vision is no real alternative. The dualist's stance separates us from our origin, whereas the origin calls us to participate in it. Interfused with goodness within the metaxological ethos, Desmond says, we are to become archaeologists of the good. We must dig to find our origin. Dwelling on the horizon, the intersection of earth and sky, we are grounded in a sense of the *elemental* that is both a part of us and beyond us.[11] For we are metaphysical, which for Desmond means that we can transcend ourselves while still being in the between.

Furthermore, on this horizon we are at the meeting point of two axes: the horizontal and the vertical. Surrounded on all sides by creatures and others in creation, if we are to find our origin, we must move along the vertical axis, thus transcending ourselves through ourselves.[12] Digging thus situates us vertically, and so our excavation toward the *arche* might seem to lead us downwards rather than upwards. In fact, though, this digging brings us toward the ground of being describable as *altus*, which as Desmond

---

9. See especially Augustine, *Confessions*, 1.1.

10. Desmond, *Ethics*, 163.

11. See especially Desmond, *Being*, 273–74; and Desmond, *Philosophy and Its Others*, 273.

12. The present discussion concentrates mainly on the sense of the elemental as grounding. It should not be forgotten, however, that not only earth, but also water, fire, and air speak to us, as we mindfully attend to the ways in which we experience ourselves as metaphysical.

reminds us elsewhere can mean both *high* and *deep*.[13] Our digging is so fundamentally elemental that it comprises participation with, rather than separation from, the world in which we live. Furthermore, its contact with the earth brings us not only to the profundity of our origin, but also to its loftiest heights. We may already be in contact with our ground, but we must penetrate its surface, in order both to explore its depths and to find its farthest-reaching significance. If we see the origin as solely above, we risk severing ourselves from it, so that it becomes irrelevant to the way we experience the world and live our lives. However, in digging to find our roots, we allow ourselves to see that the origin is already ingrained within us, in our very marrow. Through our seeking to find it, it incorporates itself more and more fully into ourselves. In digging toward it, we can see it as the ground of all: not so much a distant goal as an ever-abundant source.

For Desmond, this archaeology stands in contrast to other images of earth, especially in *Ethics and the Between*, throughout his discussion of ethical ways. Our path to the good is already somewhat articulated, because it is our ground, but some ways of inquiry can disclose themselves as derivative and closed off when they resist moving deeper and deeper downward. For example, Desmond presents us with an alternative image of a cave in contrast to Plato's allegory. *Univocity* alone cannot give voice to the ultimately unfathomable depths of the metaxological ethos, and so, Desmond says, "we must seek to build another ladder of thought in [the equivocal mud of the ethos], and up it climb; or [univocally] open a cave into the mud, a cavern into whose gloom we must climb down."[14] We can immediately note that here "climbing down" is not to go back to the cave once we have seen the *Agathon*. Nor is it to be an archaeologist looking only for the historical past understood along its horizontal trajectory. This one can compare with the univocal man's cave, which puts the real quest for goodness at an end. He builds a dwelling place in the darkness, so as to go no further. Thus he uses the gift of the ground as given to close himself off from the richness of the elementally giving source. The univocal way inward is not the way up. Rather it is a perversion of the Augustinian movement from exterior to interior, for univocal interiority is claustrophobic. It closes off any access to the divine by giving its own univocal answers, and thus pulls in the ladder to the superior solely inwards, and upon itself.[15]

---

13. Desmond, *Desire*, 199.
14. Desmond, *Ethics*, 77.
15. It should be emphasized that the metaxological does not preclude the univocal

The univocal needs instead to be tempered by the *equivocal*, in order to escape from its ossified walls by mixing life-giving water with them, giving a foundation for the equivocal. The equivocal is more akin to the metaxological, but is still not enough to allow us to appreciate what it is to transcend ourselves and thus relate back to the agapeic origin. Equivocity creeps in and clings to our boldest attempts to pin down the nature of the metaxological. As Desmond also argues, God sows confusion[16] into the matrix of the world in which we live. Traditional attempts to give voice to the ethos can forget this confusion, *undermine* it in effect, so that ethical norms become sedimented, encrusted, incapable of breathing life into real appreciation of ethical values. Thus Plato must interrogate such univocal appraisals of norms through the questioning voice of Socrates. Says Desmond:

> Tradition supposedly shows the sedimented univocities of valuation, passed on thoughtlessly from the past. To say that these univocities ('values') must be desedimented means, in part, that they must be uprooted from the *sedes*, their seat, their sediment, their soil. Tradition, as the social context of generally accepted univocities, must be called into question.[17]

Equivocal Socratic questioning seeks to restore nurturing power to values all but lost, to breathe back into the earth its life force. In a move unimaginable to Socrates, we might say that such breath derives its power from the very beginning of humanity as told in *Genesis*, where God breathed life into Adam, himself formed out of earth. This *humus*, inseparable from our humanity, can only speak to us in our metaphysical nature because of the life that sustains it. Again, we can think of this elementally, so that our incarnate nature offers a source of meaning, rich *because of* its double signification. The flesh alone cannot manifest us to ourselves. Rather, the breath that makes this flesh live opens us out toward the ultimate value of being.[18] Univocities of valuation sever value from the breath that gives it

---

(or for that matter, the equivocal and dialectical) expressions of our being in the world. Univocity here is characterized only negatively, but Desmond speaks of a more open univocity, which is directly related to our present concerns, though not discussed in the present chapter. Rapturous univocity "corresponds to the lived immediacy of our being enveloped in the pure 'stuff' of being." Desmond, *Ethics*, 273. This is not univocity as rational abstraction, but as lived harmony within the elemental world.

16. Desmond, *Ethics*, 79–82.
17. Desmond, *Ethics*, 80.
18. This refers in particular to the *passio essendi* as it is discussed in Desmond, *Ethics*;

life: the breath of God, the origin. The strength of Socrates is that he moves beyond any implosive sense of traditional norms, any way of mindlessly accepting what has been given. Plato's Socrates moves beyond the whole, by first appreciating that seeing the *Agathon* necessitates going down to the Piraeus, into the darkness of Hades, and back into the cave. Similarly, in Desmond's Augustinian odyssey, we must go down, like the ancient Greek hero visiting the underworld, before we can appreciate the transformative words of *Genesis*, "Let there be light." Only by first approaching the mystery of our source can we see the elemental nature of an affirmation that is, by its very nature, good.

The metaxological archaeologist, then, sees the real value of an equivocal mode of discovery, and digs beyond the space carved out by the univocal cave-dweller; but in his refusal genuinely to articulate this quest, the archaeologist's excavation is in peril. Realizing this jeopardy, the archaeologist may be tempted to turn to a dialectical mode, but this too is inadequate to a proper archaeology of the good. While the dialectical approach may offer a means to understand the workings of determinacy and indeterminacy, it comes to a dead end. Unable to do justice to erotic sovereignty, it cannot explain the goodness of the origin, and of being itself. Erotic sovereignty at its best is an affirmation of the self in interrelationship with others.[19] Here the person progresses erotically, from lack toward fulfilment. Here too one is sovereign because with (and even through) others, one has found oneself. Emphasis on openness is essential if we are to live up to the infinitely open source that makes erotic sovereignty possible. Erotic sovereignty, according to the dialectical approach, is infinite desire that cannot mirror its source, and so is incapable of explaining that it is simply good to be. The dialectic cannot bring us to our agapeic origin. It works toward an end, one of self-revelation and self-determination; but it can reconfigure, so as to effectively distort, the otherness of being as other, and most importantly the ultimate otherness of the source. Dialectic, especially in the hands of Hegel, works toward full disclosure, whereas attunement to the metaxological entails

---

see in particular 367 for a discussion of how God is in the "muck" or the "humus." God gives life through his breath. This constant divine invigoration is the ground for our knowledge of the goodness of being, enabling us to undergo that goodness metaphysically, which means to know it elementally, including by means of suffering as personal experience of transcendence.

19. The shortcomings of erotic sovereignty for leading the good life are articulated in part 3 of this book, through and with an examination of the demands that agapeic service places on those in the *metaxu*.

being mindfully aware of mystery. The dialectical sense that the true is the whole, and that in the end we will see this whole, is opposed to the nature of the origin as agapeic. Its giving never ends, and so neither can our appreciation of it as gift. This means that we can never hold to the idea of a "block creation."[20] The metaxological archaeologist cannot rest with such a bounded understanding. Instead, the archaeologist needs to communicate the ground of its dynamism.

This communication is possible because of the forms in which the ground communicates itself to us. For Desmond, this occurs in several ways,[21] but we are here concerned with how it takes place *elementally*, that is, through the *idiocy of being*,[22] whereby we are in immediate contact with others and the world. Without proving the surplus of the good, for this would be impossible, we dwell with it in "an initially unarticulated intimacy."[23] The idiocy of being is *metaphysical*: it inscribes itself in us while still being beyond us, and does so best elementally, as our elemental, incarnate bodies manifest ourselves to ourselves as metaphysical, as being both here and beyond ourselves. Desmond's example of this is that of weeping in grief, whereby we are overcome, without being able to explain why, and this overcoming expresses itself physically, both by and through us. Weeping—and laughing too—express what Desmond refers to elsewhere as our *passio essendi*.[24] Namely, we are given to ourselves, our flesh communicating ourselves to ourselves, in manifesting valuable aspects of being

---

20. Desmond, *Ethics*, 164.

21. There are also hyperboles, which remind us of the excess of being so we are "thrown above" ourselves. This is again the paradoxical meaning of metaphysical *grounding* as metaxological. Our ground makes us exceed ourselves, while still maintaining contact with our world. We are more fully ourselves when we transcend ourselves. For further discussion of the hyperboles, see Desmond, *Being*, 217–22; Desmond, *Ethics*, 511–13. References to the hyperboles of being are throughout *God and the Between*; see in particular chapter 7, "God Beyond the Between," 159–69. See also Tutewiler, "On the Cause." Desmond, *Intimate Strangeness*, 251–59 deals with hyperboles of being in ways that will be discussed further in chapter 4 of the present volume.

22. For Desmond's discussions of the *idiocy of being*, see, for example, Desmond, *Philosophy and Its Others*, 282–84 and 303–11; *Being*, 379–84 and 410–15; *Ethics*, 10–11 and 170–78. *God and the Between* again contains discussions throughout; the reader might consult 180–84, where discussions of flesh, family, and idiocy of being pertain to discussions in part 3 of the present volume. See also *Intimate Universal*, chapter 5: "The Idiotics of the Intimate Universal," 201–50. Also see Desmond, "Hyperbolic Thoughts."

23. Desmond, *Ethics*, 170.

24. See in particular chapter 12 of Desmond, *Ethics*: "Seventh Ethical Selving: Released Freedom and the Passion of Being," 365–84.

we cannot fully rationally understand.[25] Weeping again refers us back to the overabundance of our source, which allows us to love in ways beyond our understanding. Without love, there would be no grief. This love, issuing from the agapeic good, is further intimation to us that there is a good beyond anything we might see to be good or evil. Grief, in calling for us to affirm being even out of a sense of desolation, indicates the enigma that is our origin. This origin is intimately present and, whether communicated in joy or in despair, is primarily self-giving goodness. Thus, it is not remote from us, either as a far-off beginning point or as a distant finite end.

To reiterate, then, within Desmond's understanding of our movement toward the agapeic origin, which is our true and infinite end, there are two main Augustinian strains. Firstly, we see that the progression forms an erotic transformation of infinite restlessness into peace found in an actually infinite source. Secondly, our elemental worth issues from the intrinsically good gift of being, and we experience this in a fundamentally life-affirming incarnational manner. To accentuate these points further, we turn now to the thought of Augustine, who anticipates and elaborates, in particular upon a paradoxical and *non-linear* sense of origin; he does this especially when he meditates on the origin of the universe as told in *Genesis*. For him, the original moment of creation resonates throughout the entirety of the universe, but most especially in the human heart. Persons, unlike other creatures, have the unique opportunity actually to make incarnate the Word—present at the beginning and still resonating throughout all that exists—within themselves. Thus, conversion becomes a new creation. In effect, it is through his moment of conversion that Augustine comes to understand the workings of God *within* creation. In throwing himself down on the ground of his garden, shedding tears in his anguish before conversion, he opens in himself the possibility for life in the wasteland he has become.[26] His grief is united with that of creation yearning to be redeemed.

---

25. When I first wrote this chapter, William Desmond gave me a draft to read of a paper that had not as yet been published, "The Body Beside Itself: On Weeping and Laughing." Since then, that paper has been published in Desmond, *Gift of Beauty*, as chapter 9, "Redeeming Laughter: On the Body Beside Itself and the Passion of Being," 277–322. For Desmond, both weeping and laughing show our metaphysical relationship to the body as it manifests our transcending of purely rational modes of self-knowledge. For further reflection on what it means for the body to be beside itself, see also Augustine, *Confessions*, 8.7, where Augustine describes God turning Augustine around so that he can see himself in his depravity. This is just before Augustine's conversion, when Ponticianus is speaking to him of others who have already converted to Christ.

26. Weeping holds a significant place in Augustine's *Confessions*, as he seeks to

In terms of the saint's later explanations, Augustine longs to be *reformed*, or converted. For in the beginning, he later says in *The Literal Meaning of Genesis*, whenever God uses the word *fiat*, or "Let there be . . . ," he allows for the freedom of possibility for everything created to turn back to him.[27]

Thus a creature can tend toward nothingness or annihilation; or it can turn back to its origin and become truly formed, perfected in the light of divine love. Conversion for Augustine means fulfilment of being in a way that leaves no room for nihilism. As Desmond also holds, affirmation of the very goodness of creation is the essential response to nihilism. Like Augustine, he takes a metaphysical stance toward goodness. Thus, in *Being and the Between*,[28] he stresses that creation holds magnificent value, because it is good. This affirmation has ancient roots, but more is at stake here than tradition. When we say, as Desmond so often does throughout *Ethics and the Between*, "it is good," we give personal testimony to the overabundant gift of being. With such transformation of the will, we can turn back to the very beginning of creation.

---

understand his own heart. Early in the work, after the unnamed friend of his youth has died, he says that bitter tears replace his love for his friend. There follows a meditation on whether tears are by nature sweet or bitter, an expression of hope, a prayer, or else a reaction of revulsion, as expression of the realization that the object lost was never really properly loved (Augustine, *Confessions*, 4.4–5). When describing his conversion (Ibid., 8.12), Augustine reflects again upon the meaning of tears, which he describes as *acceptabile sacrificium tuum*, quoting Psalm 51:17, which refers to the broken heart and spirit as more acceptable to God than a holocaust. Desmond quotes this line from the *Confessions* as the epigraph to *God and the Between*, a point that is discussed in Chapter 3 of the present volume. Monica's tears are also significant within the *Confessions*. At 3.11, Augustine speaks of Monica's prayers as prayers for him, watering the ground of every place she went. The next chapter in *Confessions* recounts the story of Monica begging a bishop to reason with Augustine. The bishop is at first polite and tactful, not wanting to speak with Augustine, yet wishing to comfort his mother. Finally, in exasperation, he says to the weeping woman that the son of such tears will not perish. Here, then, Monica's tears are prayers for her son. When Augustine tells us of Monica's death and funeral, he again meditates upon weeping, in this instance his inability to weep immediately, or even during his mother's funeral (Ibid., 9.12). He wants to weep, and yet feels that this would be inappropriate at the death of a woman of such faith. Even when the time would be fitting for him to shed tears in public, he cannot, and this also is a source of consternation. Finally he cries himself. Monica had shed so many tears for him that this once he feels he can fittingly do the same in the face of her loss.

27. Augustine, *Literal Meaning*, 4.9.

28. For this discussion, see Desmond, *Being*, 505–14. This theme is also very much present in Desmond, *Art, Origins*; and again in Desmond, "Hyperbolic Thoughts."

Yearning for this same conversion of will, Augustine in the garden is longing for perfection of salvation, in communion with his origin. He wants to turn back to the beginning, making it at the same time his destination. Again, though, he understands none of this in strictly linear terms. Conversion is an ever new creation, so that he can exclaim later in the text, "Late have I loved you, beauty so ancient and so new, late have I loved you!"[29] Christ as the origin of the whole of creation is more ancient than the earth, within whose domain Augustine seeks his maker; but he is new with the selfsame vitality present at the first moment of creation. This newness *reincarnates* itself within Augustine, when he willingly makes Christ's flesh his own.[30] For the saint, this incarnation of Christ within the self—the only true selving—is quite literal, grounded in a robust sense of the elemental. In fact, Augustine's metaxological mindfulness constantly indicates his repulsion at a dualism that would separate him from the truths of the maker manifest in creation. Too often is it forgotten that Augustine's life after conversion to Christianity (and his corpus of written work expresses this) is actively opposed to any Manichaean tendency. While the Manichaeans hold that that there is a radical split between goodness and creation, such that creation is the very incarnation of evil, Augustine sees such great continuity between Creator and creation that no such dualism can be maintained. For him, instead, there is dynamic continuity between flesh and spirit, and this implicatedness of one into the other ultimately receives its surplus value from the Incarnation of Christ.

Thus, while Augustine claims citizenship in the City of God, this does not mean that he ignores or even neglects the created order. Instead, after his conversion, his vision is transformed. Previously, everything in the world seemed hateful to him. He could find no place of proper rest within

---

29. Augustine, *Confessions*, 27: *Sero te amavi, pulchritude tam antiqua et tam nova, sero te amavi!* Compare with Pine-Coffin's translation: "I have learnt to love you late, Beauty at once so ancient and so new! I have learnt to love you late!"

30. Augustine explicitly expresses this at the end of the *Confessions*, in a statement that refers back to his own conversion. At that moment in the text, at 8.12, he quotes Romans 14:11, the passage he reads when a child's voice cries *tolle lege*, telling him to put on Christ (*induite Dominum Iesum Christum*). This means transformation of the flesh as a rejection of concupiscence. Also in book 8, he refers to his conversion as conceiving in the Spirit. Augustine has a fundamentally elemental sense of how conversion refers back to the initial moment of creation. It is a new creation, which means not the rejection of creation in its corporeality, but transformation of the physical. Augustine's flesh is changed because his spirit is renewed, and because of this he can begin to see the world as God first saw it, as good.

the world, no real solace in any finite earthly pleasure. Now, with newly opened eyes, he can see the beauty of a universe striving toward the one who formed it. When our love is properly ordered, so too will be our vision of the world. In fact, our love of God intensifies our love of creation, by setting it in its proper order. This vision sees that our end is our moment of origin. This moment is for Augustine an especially personal one, because it is in effect our meeting with the person of Christ. At that point, which we call the beginning, says Augustine, the Son of God was—or better said, is—present in two ways. He is coeternal with the Fatherand Spirit; and at the same time through him all is created, in such a way that at the very moment of coming into being, creation is called to something more. Conversion entails receiving the form that was spoken perfectly in God, but perfectly in us—so that cooperation between us and the Word could come to its fullness, in the fullness of time.[31] Thus God the Son is the Creator of the possibility of the fullness of creation, by means of a call which is inseparable from himself, and which speaks the world into existence, while at the same time bidding its return. This turning back of creation is not simply the completion of a circle, so that as soon as beginning and endpoint meet, a point of stasis is reached and a kind of closure attained that needs no further movement. This reformation is instead the recognition that the transcendent breaks into and through the world in which we live. The dynamics of desire, as Desmond describes them through three forms of infinitude, point to this. Instead of closure, such that the ultimate is rejected for a form of immanent transcendence, motion, the life of the creature, is transformed and intensified. Augustine's maxim "love, but be careful what you love"[32] acknowledges that the objects of our love define us. The converted heart loves God, its will becoming more like that of the Creator. As agapeic, then, this love does not close off the possibility of loving creation. Instead, in its all-embracing nature, it allows us to see creation as it really is,

---

31. Augustine, *Literal*, 1.4,9.

32. This is the translation in Arendt, *Love and Saint Augustine*, 17. The Latin reads: *amate, sed quid ametis videte* (*Enarrations*, 31.5), and thus asks us to be watchful over what we love. Augustine asks that we love with the open eyes of a visionary who sees the goodness of being because of the nature of his origin. The world is not loved solely for itself, which would be *cupiditas*. *Caritas* breaks free of such darkened understanding. God has made us to love, but to love him first, and through him the world. This new sight is again, therefore, a participation in creation. Through Christ we are remade, just as through him, in the beginning, the world was made.

in its beauty showing us vibrant and various images of the Creator's mind. Thus Augustine says too,

> All things, after all, have in them a certain worth or grace of nature, each of its own kind, so that in these minute creatures there is even more for us to wonder at as we observe them, and so to praise the almighty craftsman for them more rapturously than ever. Indeed he made all things in the Wisdom who *reaches from end to end and sweetly disposes all things* (Wis 8:1) . . .[33]

In this new understanding of an economy of grace, of an interior more than an exterior power, Augustine says that he finds "we are more amazed at the agile flight of a fly than at the stamina of a sturdy mule on the march; and the cooperative labors of tiny ants strike us as far more wonderful than the colossal loads that can be carried by camels."[34] Such attention to the details of the workings of the world were previously only important to Augustine as rhetorical devices. Now they are further evidences, intensifications, of his awareness of the elemental, made possible because love of something finite is no longer an end in itself. End is rather bound to end, not as a measure of extent, but as a unification of communicative power. Augustine's love strives now to be as infinite and self-giving as its source, so that in loving God he loves creation both unabashedly and limitlessly.

How then are we to understand such love, which allows for no simple form of rest, but which rather is transformed by its new directedness into an outwardly embracing sense of the wholeness of creation? We must turn primarily to Augustine's sense of origin, which is at the center of his own life, while underlying the entire cosmos. This origin is paradoxical, so it cannot be expressed in any, humanly speaking, temporal or spatial terms. The limitations of human experience and knowledge deem that we form the places in which we live, and the time by which we calculate, according to boundaries set and passed. Such cannot be the case for our origin, and this very paradox is indicated in the structure of Augustine's *Confessions*.[35] The origin is at the beginning and the end of this text; but it is also at what is, spatially speaking, roughly its *center*, the moment of the saint's conversion.

---

33. Augustine, *Literal*, 3.14,22.

34. Augustine, *Literal*, 3.14,22.

35. There are various interpretations as to the cause of the structure of the *Confessions*. Key for appreciating how creation and conversion work together for Augustine, building on community and having cosmic significance, are Fiedrowicz, "Introduction"; and Vessey, "Conference and Confession."

Thus Augustine begins the work with a meditation on how we are to know God, asking whether our praise or our knowledge of him should come first. This temporal problem gives way to a meditation on the Creator's spatial relationship to the world. Augustine hence asks how God is in creation, in our lives, and yet beyond it and us. That is, he inquires into the metaphysical underpinnings of the created order, which in grounding us allows us to move beyond ourselves, back to ourselves, and thus to our true center. The last paragraph of the work plays out again the Augustinian dynamics of rest. Where God sees everything, as he has made it, from eternity, we come late to the panorama of creation. Thus at first we do evil, but when our hearts conceive by the Spirit, we are able to do good. Augustine goes on to ponder prayerfully that it is through God that we find our rest; and God is his own rest.[36] Thus in seeking God, in imitating him, we become increasingly aware that we can never find rest as mere stasis, because we can never achieve that rest which is God's own. Our rest comes from God, just as everything that we are comes from him. Having converted, then, we may recognize our origin. To put on the flesh of Christ, however, means to know that within creation our love imitates the self-giving surging power of the created order. This life came first through the Word, of whom all our finite words or actions are at least derivative, and at most imitative.

The beginning and the end of the *Confessions* are, of course, impossible for Augustine without its center, which is the moment of conversion. Thus Christ, the Word, is at the center of the work, which concentrates itself in Augustine's inner movements of the heart. This movement is a *microcosmic* manifestation of the whole account of creation. It is a particular showing forth of the way that the origin grounds, so as to allow for the peacefulness that reveals itself in an almost overwhelming activity, in a constant showing of love of God in works. From this center we can extend back toward the beginning, where Christ is too, as the Word through whom all receive life. The very start of the work asks how we can pray to God, if we do not know him. Is it through praising that we come to know him, he asks? The answer seems to be in the words of the *Confessions*, which delve into the mysterious personal workings of the Creator in one particular human life. The *Confessions*, as an archaeology of the good, is a work of memory. The fiery force of Augustine's conversion[37] sheds such light upon the whole of his thought

---

36. Augustine, *Confessions*, 13.38.53.

37. This fire, it should be noted, is the fire of the weight of love for God. For Augustine, every created thing has its own proper weight. This weight is the fire of divine love,

that he can see how the Creator has always already prepared the way for him to come to know how Christ is within him. This light spreads too toward the end-limit of the work, as its final pages explore the initial moment of creation, delving into the meaning of the words of *Genesis*, which show *macrocosmically* the Incarnation of Christ the Word in the works of creation. The origin is then at the beginning and at the end of Augustine, only because Christ is at the center, as limitless source.

If one might be so bold, then, to speak of an Augustinian odyssey in the wake of Desmond, what we would have is a ground that continually reverberates, throughout the whole of creation, stable in its dynamism, constant in its eternally issuing agapeic love. Augustine's counter to infinite restlessness is not non-activity, but rather a sense of fulfilment that answers to its source in open-ended and constant selving. His sense in the *Confessions* is that the Word through whom all things were made continues to resound throughout the created cosmos. Thus, he says, "in your Word there is no cessation of succession . . . you speak all that you speak simultaneously and eternally, and whatever you say shall be comes into being."[38] Thus, the eternal speaking of the Word sustains everything in the created order. This does not mean that our finite words are meaningless, but that we must strive to have them approach the richness of their source. In turning back toward the origin, we are transformed, and so are our words, which include not only verbal communication but also all of our various modes of communication with world, others, and ultimately with God.

Thus, before conversion, the only possibility of true selving, we could do little better than to follow Augustine, falling on the ground to water it with our tears, for this elementally expressed need for our origin is a prayer for the grace of salvation. This plea, once answered, is not the end but rather the beginning; of a life of digging back to the origin from which we were formed. It is fitting, then, that the first words of *Genesis* are *en arche*. As archaeologists, we do not look back to a fixed past, but to a moment of giving that does not end. This unendingness is what Desmond calls the *overdetermination* of the good. Thinking metaxologically, we come to know the good as *arche*, moving not toward complete disclosure, but toward an

---

for humans. See *Confessions* 13.9. This is the fire of *caritas*, which contrasts with the fires with which Augustine comes to Carthage at *Confessions* 3.1. Carnal loves are affiliated with flesh that only dies. In contrast, the fire of conversion refers to the dynamism of creation, as it was in the beginning, and thus transcends any derivative fire of inferior love.

38. Augustine, *Confessions*, 11.7.9.

open wholeness.[39] This open wholeness is the peace toward which we dig as archaeologists. It is the origin to which we come back, and our return finds its best articulation in prayer.[40]

Prayer forms the ultimate porosity between persons and Creator, the greatest and most gracious communication between us and God. Such porosity is necessary because of the openness of this exchange, and its experience as gift. In prayer, we can let our thinking take a Sabbath rest[41]—as he who is so greatly to be praised communicates with us. He thus elevates us, beyond the farthest reaches of human thought. Prayer releases us, as our work is transformed through overabundant grace. In digging toward peace, we return to our origin, so that we become more fully aware of the image and likeness in which we are originally formed.

---

39. Desmond, *Ethics*, 9.

40. See Desmond, "Is There a Sabbath for Thought?" in *Is There a Sabbath?*, 312–56.

41. This is the main theme running throughout the essays in Desmond's *Is There a Sabbath?*

2

"No Block Creation"

Good and Evil in William Desmond's Augustinian Philosophy of Elemental Order

AN ELEMENTAL APPRECIATION OF creation entails acknowledging that the fundamental human experiences of goodness and of evil cannot ever fit precisely into a predominantly rationalistic philosophical or theological system. This chapter explores this claim, thereby developing a theme opened up in the previous chapter. Specifically, it will examine the implications of thinking of creation as a closed whole, instead of as a dynamic fullness constantly in communication with divine transcendence. Discussion here develops specifically through examining the idea of being elemental, as it is to be found in the work of William Desmond, and in turn influenced by Augustine's interrelated notions of creation, freedom and redemption.[1] Drawing from Augustine's understanding of intimations of divine transcendence within the world,[2] Desmond asserts the good of the "to be" of

---

1. In this work, I will mainly refer to William Desmond's *God and the Between*. I will also draw upon his works *Being*, *Ethics*, and *Philosophy and Its Others*. I will mainly take examples for Augustine from his *Confessions*. For further studies of the Augustinian resonances within Desmond's work, see Pickstock, "What Shines Between"; and the previous chapter.

2. Augustine's idea of intimacy, specifically that God is *interior intimo meo*, or more intimate to me than I am to myself, can be directly related to Desmond's understanding of the "idiocy of being" (see for instance *God and the Between*, 36.) While I do not discuss idiocy or porosity explicitly here, both are influenced by this Augustinian notion of intimacy. For a more developed articulation of Augustinian notions of porosity, read through *God and the Between*, and see chapter 3 of the present volume.

creation, without at the same time dismissing human familiarity with the existence of evil. His view of creation as a continual elemental unfolding, rather than a simply given "block," is in this respect crucial, because it allows for personal orientation, from within a deeply fissured cosmos, toward a divine origin.

Each of the main points of the following discussion is developed in relationship to experiences of the elemental (or, in the first case, of to an image of the diametrically opposed (philosophically) modern conception of our relationship to God). In this way, I hope to emphasize that persons, qua elemental creatures, cannot engage with the world solely within the constraints of narrowly defined reason. Instead, the person as a whole—imaginatively and actively—is implicated in good and evil as these are manifestly present in creation. I begin with an image of creation that serves as a counterexample to the model of creation under consideration here: that creation is a clock, left to us by a now absent clockmaker. This mechanistic image cannot do justice to the intricacies of the created order. I then discuss the idea of a "block creation," as Desmond calls it, and challenge this specifically with the attributes of elemental creation. Thirdly, attention shifts to the significance of those moments in which we feel an absence rather than a presence of goodness in our lives. Finally, the experience of the other as radically evil is examined as a key point in elemental appreciation of the real possibility of being good in the face of what cannot be rationally known in its entirety. As I conclude, for Desmond, moments in which evil, presented to us in the face and actions of the "malign(ed) other," can provoke only one response appropriate to the agapeic origin[3] of creation. Only forgiveness can be true to our source, and the ultimate meaning of anything and everything that takes place in the realm in which we find ourselves, the *metaxu*. That this response is ethical, and thus lived, is significant in that it underlines again the elemental realities of good and evil, inseparable from us as we intermediate with others, world, and ultimately God. Furthermore, true forgiveness extends beyond simple reasonability. Forgiveness refuses to explain away evil, instead defying the latter through a specific and personal elemental act of transcendent goodness.

---

3. The main senses of the *agapeic* within Desmond's work that I allude to throughout this contribution are developed in various ways throughout his works. In *God and the Between*, see especially chapter 7, but also page 59. For a discussion of the importance of the idea of agapeic origin in Desmond's work, see Simpson, *Religion, Metaphysics*, 107–10.

"No Block Creation"

God as Clockmaker: The Mechanistic Model of Creation

In order to appreciate the significance of thinking the world as elemental, it is helpful first to consider an opposing model. For this, we can turn to Desmond's *God and the Between*, where, when discussing univocal ways of thinking about God, he offers two related images that signal the dangers inherent in thinking about our relationship to God through creation only in terms of mathematical intelligibility. Modernity comes to the point, he argues, where God's relationship to what he has made is nothing more than that of a clockmaker to a clock (the world as a whole) or a watchmaker to a set of watches (where the watches are individual humans). In (post-)modernity, Desmond argues, the result of our striving to become in charge of nature is that we are left with a world devoid of goodness. Power has replaced goodness, and God, when deemed simply the most powerful of all that has power, becomes defined only in terms of having the absolute power to bring into effect.[4] Humans begin to think of God as though he is a clockmaker, says Desmond, and the inevitable result is that they think of the world as a machine. Everything about such a machine is based on power and efficiency. This is not an organic way of thinking about the world. In place of the equivocal modes of being in the world, where "life" and "love" are impossible to pin down and yet always inform a worldview, we have only "mathematical univocalizations."[5] Unlike an organic life form, a machine can be dismantled and examined—interrogated, even—not in terms of goodness, but for its efficiency. Machines can, that is, be judged according to external criteria.[6] We are not dealing with a world that is good in itself. In synch with this worldview, Diderot comes to characterize humans as "walking watches" and we then think of God as an engineer working on the larger clock that is the world, with mechanised and precise "eternal geometry."[7] In such a vision, God's connections to world and humans are necessarily far removed from us. In the moment of making, the clockmaker was everything to the clock. Now, though, he is irrelevant, his presence an empty echo of a past long gone.

What more might be said of the Maker of creation, if creation is held to be like a clock and we like watches, left to be found and analyzed? To

---

4. Desmond, *God and the Between*, 63.
5. Desmond, *God and the Between*, 63.
6. Desmond, *God and the Between*, 63.
7. Desmond, *God and the Between*, 63.

be sure, these devices might be intriguing, and we could conceivably even admire the intellectual prowess and technical abilities of the one who could make them. However, when God's act of creation is seen only as a moment in the past, which has little to do with our everyday lives here and now, the result is either overt or pseudo atheism. Like Sartre the atheist, one is compelled to reject a tyrant whose very existence would divest us of all freedom. Sartre's image of God as artisan entails that nothing that the creator makes can act out of true freedom. All must be determined, because someone who makes an object always does so with a fixed nature in mind. Divine desire, inflexible from the beginning, cannot abide anything other to itself.[8] An alternate picture of creation as rationalistic and mechanistic can be found in someone like Leibniz, who wants a completely rational God. Desmond observes that such hyper-rationalism leads to its opposite: the irrationality of a world in which evil is explicable, as part of a best possible world. Here, Desmond argues, we are bereft both of freedom and of "the overdeterminacy that releases it."[9] The origin cannot speak to us out of this overdeterminacy, and so we are incapable of being open to the free givenness of being. No longer able to know that being is a gift, we become incapable of "mindfulness"; instead, reason "sleepwalks," having built up "constructions."[10] The latter explain everything, and at the same time nothing. Such constructions can be completely understood, but they leave out the very essence of being in a cosmos that sustains and communicates the goodness of being and the transcendent beneficence of a divine benefactor.[11] According to Desmond, *counterfeit doubles* of God are prevalent in (post-)modern thought.[12] Each offers something that looks like it could be divine transcendence, but which is essentially valueless and fraudulent. Leibniz the theist cannot offer a God of agapeic love, which would guarantee that the other can always be free, even to the point of coming to be evil.

Such insipid renderings of the nature of created goodness—its parts simply move, and so it *works*—have many problems. Perhaps the most striking is that they can in no way account for the elementally experienced

---

8. Desmond refers to Sartre's idea of creation as found in Sartre, *Existentialism*. See in particular Desmond, *God and the Between*, 65.

9. Desmond, *God and the Between*, 68.

10. Desmond, *God and the Between*, 68.

11. Desmond, *God and the Between*, 68.

12. See Desmond, *Hegel's God*, 9, for a discussion of Desmond's definition of "counterfeit double."

presence of evil within the world. When evil fits too neatly into a systematic account, the result can be even more dissatisfying than when it is overlooked entirely. The image whereby the world is a clock, in which we are mere cogs, or else watches mechanically going through the motions, is the picture of a universe forsaken. Perhaps it was loved when it was made, and it may even be still held in something like divine regard. But this is a God with a distant gaze and a seeming lack of interest in being involved in any way in the world that he has started up.[13] Desmond does not rule out that this counterfeit of God might need to "intervene" now and again, so that the machine-like universe keeps operating as it should.[14] However, such interventions are hardly to be understood as coming from the hand of a loving God who assures and tends directly to the freedom, development and growth of his creatures. The clock has been set, and it ticks away; it is predictable and predetermined. Here there is no space for prayer, and no possible reason for the mysterious workings of grace.

Desmond's response to the univocal picture of creation given in the rational world view can be understood via his sense of such overdeterminacy and freedom, each of which issue from an agapeic source in whose work we can participate. As Desmond says, we can actually *cooperate* in creation, becoming co-creators, by reiterating what is already present in the overdetermined source of what is. In order to approach these terms, I will now discuss Desmond's elemental appreciation of creation, which iterates views of freedom and creation very much influenced by Augustine.

Elemental Intimations of the Divine

Desmond's philosophy of the between invites one to find clues of the meaning of being, beginning with where we are, in the created order. Looking around us, in the *metaxu*,[15] between and at the same time involved in the truth that can be found there, it is fitting to say that creation is actually not completely determined. It is, instead, overdetermined. Everything that we experience offers viewpoints toward something more. Thus, at any given moment of personal involvement in creation, one is immersed in meanings of which one is both aware and unaware. No event is ever exhausted in its

---

13. See Desmond, *God and the Between*, 255.
14. Desmond, *God and the Between*, 255.
15. *Metaxu* is Desmond's term for the "middle" or the "between." See the introduction to the present volume.

implications, for: "[i]n creation beings are not completely constituted from the outset. They are in process of becoming themselves. So they are not completely coincident with themselves."[16] Taking together the values inherent in the goodness of creation in its constant becoming, one can derive insight into the array of ways in which divine presence is uttered throughout creation. Overdetermination, that is, entails not thinking of creation as a "block," made and let alone with no possibility to strive beyond.[17] As William Desmond says in *Ethics and the Between*,

> . . . this is no block creation. There is a pluralism to creation, reflected in the pluralism of original powers marking different beings. The good of beings is shown in the ontological integrity, out of which a being's powers emerge into expression, and shown in the harmony of wholeness it seeks to attain in fulfilling these its powers.[18]

Creation may well display some kinds of uniform attributes, but it is by no means static.

We are, then, by nature of an elemental order that is constantly rearranging itself, as its finite members shift into and out of being as humans know it in the world. For Desmond, creation constantly announces an order of goodness; this is also the case for Augustine, who emphatically echoes Saint Paul's claim that anyone who cannot find signs of God when wondering at and meditating upon creation is "without excuse."[19] Here it is particularly helpful to describe some of the main attributes of the elemental in relationship to the elemental philosophy present in the thought of Augustine. In this way we can come closer to elucidating what precisely is at stake in Desmond's elemental, metaxological[20] vision of creation. Specifically, Augustine sustains the value of all that is created, while at the same time doing justice to the confusing nature of that same world's chiaroscuro of being. To speak in Desmond's terms, Augustine does so by emphasizing the relationship of divine transcendence to the world, in its agapeic, overdetermined intermediations. I will here call upon both Augustine and

---

16. Desmond, *Being*, 279.
17. See Desmond, *God and the Between*, 168.
18. Desmond, *Ethics*, 164.
19. Augustine, *Confessions*, 10.8. Augustine is quoting Romans 1:20. References to the *Confessions* throughout this volume refer to the Boulding translation unless stated otherwise.
20. See the introduction to the present volume, and also Desmond, *Being*, xii.

Desmond to describe what is at stake in being elemental. While focus in this section is on the ways in which the elemental specifically conveys the goodness of being, it serves as a precursor to discussion in the next, final section, which deals with how freedom within elemental creation is the key to understanding experiences of darkness, of despair, and even of radical evil within the *metaxu*. This same freedom is vital to the possibility of forgiveness, which can be gainfully compared with Augustine's appreciation of the reality of redemption.

Augustine's approach to the elements is metaxological in that it begins precisely in the *between*, within the world in which we already live. We too are caught up in that world, and can, like him and with Desmond, find that our relationship to divine transcendence is essentially of an elemental order. The elemental can be thought in two ways. First, it can be understood literally in terms of earth, air, fire and water. Secondly, one can think of the elemental as the involvement of the whole person in creation. In the latter instances, one is taken up into an experience of the world that can never be exhausted in its known intelligibility. That is, the elemental constantly surprises and always exceeds us. These modes announce themselves emphatically at certain unexpected moments, which abruptly pull us up to face the reality that we are predisposed to respond to the primordial goodness of Creator and creation.

To know the first way of approaching the elemental, we can turn to Augustine's discussion in Book X of his *Confessions*, where he speaks of his experience of earth, air, fire and water, each in terms of its particular and idiosyncratic aspects. He calls upon each in turn: the earth, "the sea and the great deep and the teeming live creatures that crawl," "the gusty winds, and every breeze with all its flying creatures" and "the sky . . . sun, moon, stars." They are so compelling in their majesty that he "puts [his] question" to them, begging "Tell me of my God . . . You are not he, but tell me something of him." Each in its own way points him beyond. These elements, who stand "around the portals of [his] flesh," "[lift] up their mighty voices and [cry] 'He made us.'"[21] Augustine hears each reply in its own voice, with what he says is their unique mark of the beauty, which the creator is still bestowing. But in order for him to hear that response, he must foster proper receptiveness. This, his "attentive spirit," is his openness to the otherness of creation, which has everything to tell him about himself, about what it is to be of the created order. Similar attentiveness is at work throughout Desmond's work.

21. Augustine, *Confessions*, 10.9–10.

For instance, in *God and the Between*, among other descriptions he relates how we constantly use our senses, and how touch in particular brings us into contact with the cosmos as it transmits life and love.[22] Elsewhere in the same work he muses on how the world communicates itself to us through the ways that we experience its equivocal immediacy. This has aesthetic dimensions: we are erotically drawn toward the beauty of the world, not only through "sexual eros" but via such experiences as breathing in the air of a summer morning, living in unison with the "aesthetic show of creation."[23]

The metaxological sensibilities that Augustine and Desmond both express derive from their shared capacity to learn from the dynamism and diversity of the elements. Such ways of being and expression also convey that a person continues to learn from and grow together with the ways of creation. All that is created, says Desmond, is constantly "coming to be."[24] Likewise, in Augustine's descriptions, each of the elements is engaged in some kind of activity. For Desmond, creation is perpetually in transition, and yet, far from disorienting and displacing us, its elemental movement "is transition as vector of transcendence. Creation as universal impermanence, as it were, reaches beyond its open wholeness to its own transcendent ground."[25] Thus, creation is dynamic, rather than static; and this dynamism indicates the nature of its transcendent ground as actively participating in everything as it comes to be. Elemental creation offers resources through which to know our relationship to transcendent being. Like us, the elements are filled with movement and life. Like us too, each element in its unique way of being, in its constant and astonishing unfolding of selfhood, expresses something of the goodness of creation.

However, there is another aspect of the elemental which is quintessentially human, not shared by the elements. Unlike us, the elements do not experience perplexity; and they cannot practice the same mindful cooperation with creation to which persons are intimately called. Humans, that is, have the capacity to rise above finite concerns, to appreciate and enrich intermediations of divine transcendence within the world. The second way of appreciating what it means to be elemental can bring the latter points more clearly to the fore. It is not imperative that the second way of being elemental explicitly include one of the four primary elements. Instead,

---

22. Desmond, *God and the Between*, 17.
23. Desmond, *God and the Between*, 75.
24. See especially Desmond, *God and the Between*, 248–50.
25. Desmond, *Being*, 293.

being elemental in this sense means complete involvement in the world's ways of signifying transcendence: moments of elemental awareness can be fleeting. They are, though, no less startling for that, and they tend to awaken perplexity and wonder at the constant incarnations of goodness within creation. Desmond considers:

> Most often these communications are godsends that come quietly. The agapeics of the divine arrive unobtrusively in the most hidden of elemental things: a mustard seed, a smile, a song, a glint of sun, a drink of pure water, a child holding one's hand, the comfort of fire on a bitter day, the uninsistent aid of an agapeic servant.[26]

In themselves, each of these is seemingly insignificant, even appearing as nothing. Unless we attend to what each has to say about the transcendent source, they are indeed cast into a realm of nothingness. However, each has the capacity to remind that we are enmeshed in a world in which everything that exists has excessive, overdetermined meaning, derived from its source, which is overabundant and good. Each is, in fact, a concrete member of the community of creation of which we are members. Like other creatures, we are created.

What we find in creation and the ways that it affects and moves us indicates not a univocal God who sets the world in stone and leaves it alone, but instead a creator who makes in ways that enmesh creatures entirely in their made milieu, if the same creatures be willing to do so. In other words, if we not only look at but become completely involved in the world, we can find what is transcendent to, and yet somehow intimated within, the dynamic order in which we live. The significance of the elemental, then, is that it can bring us closer to knowing its source—which means also our own source. It makes no sense by such a reckoning to insist on a model of creation that has little or nothing to do with us or with God. In Desmond's terms again, we are not living in or dealing philosophically with a "block creation," made once and then ignored. Augustine, too, expresses joy and astonishment at the varieties of praise that creation offers to its transcendent source. Every creature is to him a sign of the worthiness of what has been made, but also of God, the Creator's love. Nonetheless, both Augustine and Desmond describe and account for moments when goodness is not so readily apparent. It is to these that we now turn, so as to find the

---

26. Desmond, *God and the Between*, 338.

space in which forgiveness and redemption prove to be our cooperation in the primordial work of goodness in creation and in our lives.

Agapeic Love, Human Freedom, and the Elemental Problem of Evil

The overdeterminacy of creation makes itself felt not only in affirmative moments of elemental experience. In experiences of a more negative ilk, one can begin to discern how the elemental speaks of the nature of evil and the appropriate human response to its instantiations in the world. Augustine's *Confessions* offers a vast range of examples of the strange ways in which evil insinuates itself in our lives, and by that fact whispers about an agapeic source. Throughout that work, without quite understanding why, Augustine feels physically and emotionally overcome with a sense of disorientation. Whether he is wantonly and without reason throwing pears to pigs;[27] yearning for the grace of conversion of the will;[28] weeping at the loss of his mother;[29] or declaring that his transformative love for the Lord has come too late,[30] Augustine expresses heartfelt longing that no univocal, rational system can explain away. What Desmond in turn calls "being at a loss" Augustine accounts for in theological terms as a result of original sin. Desmond speaks in philosophical terms about *creatio ex nihilo*. To be sure, this formulation has theological ancestry and ties. Nonetheless, considering it in terms of being and of non-being, brings to light that it is also squarely within the main area of metaphysical discourse.

This way of thinking creation cannot be confined to univocal discourse, but instead calls for terms of elemental intercommunication. Within a vibrant picture of the elemental, one cannot deny those moments of lack, felt when something of the nothingness out of which creation has been made creeps into moments of our everyday lives. Desmond describes explicitly, saying:

> we must consider a more radical sense of indeterminate nothing. Something of it is 'manifest' in our encounter with radical evil. It is intimated in the mortality of beings, beings marked by the

---

27. Augustine, *Confessions*, 2.9.

28. Augustine, *Confessions*, 8.19.

29. Augustine, *Confessions*, 9.33. For the significance of weeping throughout the *Confessions*, see previous chapter, note 26.

30. Augustine, *Confessions*, 10.38.

extraordinary singularity of their 'once.' We are touched by it when we despair: everything seems to 'come to nothing' and we ourselves 'are as nothing.' Beyond all determinate intelligibility, we experience a radical 'being at a loss.'[31]

These moments recall us to ourselves with an eeriness suggesting that the overdetermined cosmos tells not only of an agapeic source, but also of that origin's relationship to what has been made. We are reminded that without God, there is simply nothing, and that absolute reliance of all of existence on such absolute surplus is truly lived in various strange ways. Taken by surprise, we are forced to find ways to explain these unexpected inklings which threaten to be absolutely meaningless. When finite meaning is cast within the framework of an overarching intelligibility that allows us to make sense of these moments, they do not lose their peculiarity. Rather, that jarring feeling is thereby done justice, opening up ways of knowing how we experience the nothing, rather than resorting to the rationalistic option of declaring that evil is simply part of the way that the whole system works; or else that it, like everything that we encounter, makes no sense whatsoever.

Here too recourse to Augustine is helpful. Specifically his philosophy of creation opens up an overdeterminate universe of freedom, such that the Creator is both distinct from and yet intimately involved in creation. While upholding the goodness of Creator and creation, Augustine acknowledges the constant seeming presence of privation of that goodness in our everyday lives. One need not launch into an excursus about Augustine's theory of evil as privation to derive a point vital to understanding the elemental. Precisely, for Augustine, good's privation must always be put in its place. It is as nothing; next to goodness, evil even in the most radical form must turn away, blinded by the hyper-intelligibility through which all that is made constantly comes to be. The problem of theodicy, re-phrased by Desmond, is pertinent here. He asks: if God is agapeic, then how is he not somehow "complicit" in evil? After all, he lets it happen. Is he, then, holding himself back from stopping evil?[32] Such a view, though, would undermine the radical—"hyperbolic"—sense of freedom granted by agapeic love.[33]

---

31. Desmond, *God and the Between*, 244.
32. Desmond, *God and the Between*, 256.
33. See Christopher Ben Simpson's gloss on the consistency in Desmond's argument for an agapeic God *and* the existence of evil in creation: ". . . there is a conceptual consistency between the existence of an agapeic origin and the existence of evil, for a creation

Let us refer momentarily to Augustine before returning to this point within Desmond's philosophy. Namely, for Augustine, human freedom, together with the freedom of the whole created order, issues from the continual speaking of the Creator. With the words "Let there be . . . ," present in the beginning of *Genesis*, God sets into motion an entire world with the capacity to turn toward him or else to turn away.[34] This beginning is continuous for Augustine, and personal conversion is the most intense cooperation with creation. To convert is to be re-created and re-formed;[35] it is to turn away from sin in order to move with, rather than against, the currents of divine love that stream through the world. Again, this is no block creation. It has not happened once and for all, but is still uttered, for as long as creation is in existence, coming to be. This letting be of beings on the part of the Creator is, of course, no *laissez faire* attitude in the crudest sense of the term. Instead, when God lets beings be, he does not determine their existence; he allows them to unfold.

As Desmond later indicates, God lets being be other; he does not reduce otherness to manifestations of selfhood. This is an Augustinian understanding of creation, and it can be found in the following:

> In originating creatures, God communicates but reserves power to allow their power to be. God's power is *absolute* relative to the coming to be, but it is *cooperative* relative to the becoming of created beings . . . In the reserve of divine patience, the gift of freedom sometimes means allowing by doing nothing, sometimes secret rejoicing with the creature, sometimes anonymous coaxing, sometimes persuading silently. The reserve of the divine cannot be separated from the finesse: intimate companionship with the mortal creature, devotion to its good, courtesy to its singular integrity. God is esteem for the gift, honoring the promise that we are come to redeem.[36]

The elemental conveys such intimacy. It enables us not to rationalize away God's presence to us, but instead to wonder at it, even perhaps especially in those moments when evil insinuates its presence into our lives. Being at a

---

without the possibility of evil is not the result of agapeic creation, not truly other to the creator, not released, free." Simpson, *Religion, Metaphysics*, 110.

34. See Fiedrowicz, "General Introduction," 173.

35. For a more detailed discussion of the idea of reformation, especially in Augustine's *The Literal Meaning of Genesis*, see Ladner, "Saint Augustine and the Difference," 153–283; and Harrison, "Measure, Number, and Weight."

36. Desmond, *God and the Between*, 257.

loss can tempt us to deny the very existence of superabundant goodness. It is then, though, that nothingness begins to feed upon itself. The only antidote to the meaninglessness that such experience of nothingness implies is in turning to the surplus of meaning that constantly runs through our very pores, and yet remains in its entirety beyond our grasp.

What then can we make of evil, intimated to us radically and otherwise in our elemental ways of being in the world? How does the vision of an overdeterminate creation constantly issuing from an agapeic source account for its presence? Such a picture, in sharp contrast to the theistic picture of the abandoned clock, constantly exceeds any determinate statements we might make about it. The world slips away from any attempt at conceptual reach, as our mindfulness strives to catch up with moments of intense elemental awareness. This way of being asks that we view the seeming presence of evil with a spirit that goes beyond any bare concept. Specifically, it calls not only toward a way of rational knowing, but also of being and of acting. Any recognition of evil demands the seemingly paradoxical personal acknowledgement that goodness is the source. Without goodness, evil would be unrecognizable.

That is, radical evil, acknowledged for what it is, calls us to forgive, in this way allowing us to move with, rather than against, the source of our elemental awakenings and unquenchable perplexities. Such forgiveness is the most hyperbolic and at the same time most fundamental way we can find to *cooperate* in creation. It is the most intense and intimate ethical concretion of being good. And ethics, as Desmond constantly reminds, cannot be truly thought unless it relies upon the "it is good" of creation. Perhaps it is not too much to say that for Desmond—and here too he proves very Augustinian—it is only when we find ourselves at a loss that we can discover the profundity of divine promise. While radical evil cannot fit into any systematic picture of creation, its excess can indicate the inadequacy of the finite human terms through which we strive to understand the existence of radical and seemingly absolutely senseless evil. Desmond's suggestion—framed in terms of a *perhaps*—is that "Only God as absolute can suggest to us that perhaps, perhaps, what is damned for us, I mean absolutely lost, is given reprieve or another chance. Who among us can say?"[37]

What we can say, through our comportment toward the world and through that world to God, can strive toward acknowledging the possibility of that other chance. In his earlier work *Philosophy and its Others*,

---

37. Desmond, *God and the Between*, 257.

Desmond suggests that the limits of the ethical—where being ethical passes over into being religious—are to be found at the moment where we cannot understand the radical, seemingly evil, other, and yet find within ourselves the resources to forgive.[38] In *God and the Between*, he is more explicit about the potencies of forgiveness, especially in relationship to our elementally circumscribed cooperation with the divine source of everything that exists. Desmond states that when we say "It is nothing," to the one we forgive, we nullify what would otherwise be only evil. We replace "guilt and indebtedness"[39] with an assuredness in the primal divine gift of being itself. When we release an evil so that we make it into nothing, at the same time we open up a space of freedom. Gratitude is now possible, and obligation and the law are seen in light of something greater.[40] We know them, as it were, at "zero point."[41] We sense and find their origin, in a moment that does not need to happen, but that, when it does come to pass, enables us to see freedom for what it is, in relation to being.[42] Forgiveness, then, one might say, is a kind of relief, a respite within the complexity of elementally inspired hyper-awareness and perplexity. It is a glimpse of the peace for which Augustine hunts, even as it courts him, in his restless striving. That final peace, in the presence of divine transcendence, is anticipated in every moment of elemental experience. Our elemental experiences of good and of evil already indicate that this peace will be anything but monotonous. Forgiveness derives from the same source as the elemental. By entering into attentive awareness of what the elemental has to tell us, of the goodness of the "to be" and its transcendent source, forgiveness becomes possible. The finitude of created things in moments of forgiveness reveals that creation is no "block," but constantly in the process of emergence. Our cooperation, in the "vector of transcendence" where we, with creation, come to be, is the undergoing of personal redemption, the promise of which is constantly present in the primordial goodness of creation.

---

38. See especially Desmond, *Philosophy and Its Others*, 201–5.
39. Desmond, *God and the Between*, 287.
40. Desmond, *God and the Between*, 287.
41. Desmond, *God and the Between*, 30.
42. Desmond, *God and the Between*, 287.

PART 2

Becoming Porous:
The Aesthetics of Prayerful Contemplation

3

Gifted Beggars in the *Metaxu*

A Study of the Platonic and Augustinian Resonances of *Porosity* in *God and the Between*

As evidenced throughout *God and the Between*, a metaxological approach entails a richly paradoxical appreciation of how persons communicate with divine transcendence. We are to become *porous* to divine intermediations throughout the *metaxu*. That is to say, in our elemental attentiveness, we should become like beggars at the table of divine fullness: confident in the riches of divine communication; and humble and sincere enough to recognize and request them. All of this is fundamental to Desmond's grasp of the relationships between *eros* and *agape*, which is in turn indebted to the notion of our gifted and beggarly movement toward divine transcendence. The porous sensibilities of Plato and Augustine underlie the metaxological ethos from which Desmond writes; for Desmond's perspective shares much with the milieu of Plato's *Symposium*, particularly as it touches on the *daimonic* nature of *eros*; and with Augustine's admonishment that nothing that we have is ours alone and that to pray is to intensify properly oriented desire. *God and the Between* articulates the intricate interplay of thought and prayer, so that the whole work can be read as the elaboration of its epigraph from Augustine's *Confessions*: "Sacrificem tibi famulatum cogitationis et linguae meae, et da quod offeram tibi."[1] Such sacrificial offering demands that we give in return everything we have prayerfully received.

For Desmond, then, it is in attentively receiving that we live out the passion of our being, our *passio essendi*. Distinct from, but not necessarily inimical to, *conatus essendi*,[2] this receptivity enables us to communicate with God, through prayer, and through thought that at certain moments can be as gifted as prayer. As Desmond discusses often throughout *God and the Between* and elsewhere, modern philosophy's quest for absolute autonomy, in the spirit of *conatus essendi* having closed itself to the resources of *passio essendi*, severs our ties with a greater sense of what it means to be human. In *God and the Between*, Kant and Spinoza in particular come to stand for this modern urge. Desmond takes the term *conatus essendi* from Spinoza, for whom it stands for the essence of a being—the human being—who has before it infinite possibilities, with nothing to stop it from pressing forward as far as it wills to go. As Desmond warns, when the human subject becomes infinite in power and possibility, it tends to close itself off from the greater energies of selving available through what he terms a "patience of being." Attentiveness to the possibilities of the *passio essendi* can, according to Desmond, restore a truer sense of the whole of the human person, open to communications of divine transcendence in the *metaxu*. In this way we can become *porous* to the fullness of what it means to be human, and therewith elementally stirred by intermediations of divine transcendence.

Recognition of the importance of the empty fullness that comprises porosity reveals that thought and prayer are alike gifts, and that humans

---

1. Desmond, *God and the Between*, v. Cf. Maria Boulding's translation: "Let me offer in sacrifice to you the service of my heart and tongue, but grant me first what I can offer to you." This translation continues in a way extremely appropriate to the dynamics of porosity to be explored here: "for I am needy and poor, but you are rich unto all who call upon you." As we will see, this calls to mind Plato's image of *Penia* begging at the door of the feast of the gods in the *Symposium*. Interestingly too, Boulding uses the word "heart" here for *cogitationis*; for Augustine the heart is the place of our innermost and most intimate relationship with God. Cf. also the following translations, this time only of the epigraph to *God and the Between*. Rex Warner: "I want to sacrifice to you the service of my thought and of my tongue, and I beg you to give me what I may offer to you." R. S. Pine-Coffin: "Let me offer you in sacrifice the service of my thoughts and my tongue but first give me what I may offer to you."

2. For the distinction between *passio essendi* and *conatus essendi* and the importance of the *passio essendi*, cf. especially Desmond, *Ethics*, 365–84; Desmond, *Art, Origins*, 10, 288. In relation to Hegel, cf. Desmond, *Hegel's God*, 40–41, 87. Cf. also Desmond, *Is There a Sabbath?*, 23 for the relationship to porosity, chapter 9 for its relation to peace, and 245–61 for the elemental relationship of *passio essendi* to courage.

are ontologically porous. Desmond's term *porosity* recurs throughout *God and the Between* and is employed earlier in *Art, Origins, Otherness*[3] and *Is There a Sabbath for Thought?*[4] It resonates with its first meanings in the *Symposium*,[5] as well as with Augustine's understanding that prayer is the point of interior and intimate relationship to God.[6] The following discussion explores three keys to understanding Desmond's idea of porosity. First, it outlines the imagery that he uses about porosity in *God and the Between*, regarding its clogging and possibilities for unclogging. Secondly, it discusses the genesis of the term, in Plato's *Symposium*, where Socrates' disposition toward divine communication lives out Plato's notion that the intermediating path of *eros* is between mortals and gods, and likewise between poverty and resource. Finally, it articulates several key points of Augustine's philosophy of prayer, in which the intimacy of prayer supplies impetus, while thoughts expressed in words support the labor, of honing one's desire for shared immortal company with God. This passion of thought, crucial to Plato and Augustine and Desmond, would by their own accounts be impossible were it not for an underlying presence of constant divine intermediation. For all three thinkers, the divine can communicate to and through us only when we become poor in spirit, beggars yearning

---

3. See the above footnote. Cf. also Desmond, *Art, Origins*, 3: "To live as human is always to be porous to being struck by . . . astonishment and perplexity about origin."

4. See especially Desmond, *Is There a Sabbath?*, 21–25.

5. The *Symposium* is a dialogue *par excellence* of the *metaxu*, speaking as it does of love in many voices. Univocally and equivocally each speaker seeks to understand the role of *eros* as it mediates our intermediations with the world and what lies beyond. The speeches take place in the house of Agathon, and so, within the ethos of the good, and they culminate not in a closed dialectical summary of what has gone before, but in Socrates' account of his conversation with Diotima. *Eros*, Diotima says, is between the mortal and the divine, and thus not to be associated entirely with either one. Love is a half-way path. *Eros*, furthermore, seems to seek completion, and yet it is born of a plenitude that needs no other. For a metaxological reading of the *Symposium*, inspired by Desmond, see Moore, "Plurivocal Eros."

6. For a discussion of Augustine's influence on Desmond's *Ethics* and references to his explicit evocation of Augustine in various works prior to *God and the Between*, see chapter 1 of the present volume. See also Pickstock, "What Shines Between." Pickstock speaks of Desmond's influences by Plato, Augustine, and Thomas (107) and carries out an extended exploration of Augustine's sense of the meaning of light in comparison with more modern approaches to (divine) sources of knowledge. Main references by Desmond to Augustine in *God and the Between* can be found on 36, 83, 97, 157, 268, 294. Allusions to Augustinian tenets are also present in footnotes of *God and the Between*, and also, for instance: "We do not do justice to the intimate otherness of our own *passio essendi*" (22); "God [is] more intimate than life and death are to themselves" (304).

for closer relationship with what transcends. In *God and the Between*, primal porosity constantly holds sway, allowing personal acquiesence to the goodness of being, lived as the gifts of thought and prayer.

Clogging, Covering Over, Unclogging, and Sweating: Images of Porosity in *God and the Between*

Throughout *God and the Between*, Desmond repeatedly returns to the various ways, insidious or self-consciously dramatic, by which certain versions of (post-)modern rationality bring about separations between thought and prayer. Such rifts not only block passages of discourse; more importantly, they clog our ontological pores. That is to say, they alienate humans from the possibility to be open to what is present to them as transcendent. One might say that William Desmond espouses the other option open to the postmodern thinker, by responding to modern and contemporary thought, while at the same time emphasizing the possibilities to find perennial values for each person's quest for the ultimate and divine in pre-modern resources that might otherwise be neglected. At the same time, his approach recognizes that thought and prayer both issue from a rich milieu—the *metaxu*, as Desmond, drawing from Plato's use of the term in the *Symposium*, calls it—of endowed being. This gift flows from an agapeic source, and all our desires receive their motivation from that same origin. That is to say, prayer and thought, expressions of our interrelationships within the *metaxu*, are gifts bestowed by the prior gift of divine love. Porosity in this sense can be termed the predisposition to respond with a love attuned to that love first given.

To know these points better, it is helpful to examine some of the imagery Desmond uses to elaborate porosity in *God and the Between*. Clogging, unclogging, covering over and sweating each relates to the literal and figurative definitions of porosity. In its basic sense, something is porous if it allows the elements to pass through it. As one dictionary definition describes, porous means: "Full of pores; having minute interstices through which water, air, light, etc., may pass."[7] Elementally speaking, within the context of Desmond's thought, to be porous is to allow the elements to transmit in the subtlest manner possible, through spaces so small that they can be clogged or ignored, the significance of the goodness of being itself, and the agapeic nature of all that is of the *metaxu*. The elements should not be thought in

---

7. Brown, *New Shorter Oxford*, s.v. "Porous."

their physical capacities alone. The quintessentially human attribute of being elemental entails that there are inscribed within and through us ways in which the world can communicate to and with us. It is, however, not that the world speaks out of itself alone; elemental communication talks of God, and is at the same time divine speech, for God speaks to humans through everything that he constantly makes. This first sense is the way to understand porosity as ontologically human, while resourced in the divine.

The second signification is related to the figurative definition of porosity, which entails that if something or someone is porous, they are open to influences from the outside; for persons, this means allowing oneself to be passively affected so as to enable a response of befitting action. In this wise, we are open to intermediations in the *metaxu*; our thoughts and prayers are porous to each other; and philosophy and religion recognize one another as counterparts, each a rich resource rising toward and in communication with ultimacy. This notion of porosity is a keystone to Desmond's metaxological philosophy, which seeks to open up parallels as well as points of intersection between (philosophical) thought and (religious) prayer.

However, our pores can become clogged for various reasons, making such symbiotic relationships impossible. When one is open to being, one's response can comprise a spontaneous "ontological 'yes,'" which, Desmond says, "surges in and through us in the *passio essendi*."[8] The latter is our enacted porosity, at first present via what Desmond calls elsewhere "rapturous univocity,"[9] by which we sing the elemental as it moves us and passes through us. However, Desmond continues, beyond the first "ontological 'yes'" there is a second stage: it is the "either/or" whereby we need to choose either "yes" or no" in response to the goodness, the worth, of being.[10] We are free to deny the goodness of being; there is no way that reason alone can convince us to speak the "ontological yes." Affirming the goodness of being, as a happening in and through us, can be thought through in some dimensions. We can listen to "arguments and reminders,"[11] which may make us more open to receiving the elemental. And yet, these are never enough alone. The affirmation of being concerns not only argued reasons.

Furthermore, while to move toward the "no" is to clog that ontological "yes," it is not that we lose our pores altogether when we choose not to live

---

8. Desmond, *God and the Between*, 35.
9. Cf. especially Desmond, *Philosophy and Its Others*, 180.
10. Desmond, *God and the Between*, 35.
11. Desmond, *God and the Between*, 35.

the goodness of being. Instead, they become incapacitated. In these cases, even if we then know "in an abstract intellectual way"[12] that we *should* say "yes," still we cannot. Sometimes too, we may think we are living that affirmation, but we have fooled ourselves. In other words, we cannot simply reason to and decide to perform such affirmation. The latter is a happening, something received and undergone. Nonetheless, whenever we deliberately deny the ontological "yes," we become closed to the elemental speech of creation, no longer engaged in our *passio essendi*, and thus unable to speak a spontaneous affirmation of the goodness of being. Human thought and prayer alike derive from an agapeic source, which bestows the primal ethos, which "seeds a kind of urge to sing."[13] This song is not ours alone, but given and shared, with its source as well as with those who would hear.

It is telling that argument alone cannot impel an ontological "yes" or "no." Rational argument—in the modern rationalistic ethos—might certainly be a factor in the gradual clogging of pores described, but if so it is only one of several possible other causes. Affirmation or negation of the elemental "yes" reaches to the heart of the human person, which cannot be known by rationality alone. Porous philosophical thought is more than solitary reason construed in the strictly modern sense, because it draws upon reserves that cannot be completely spoken; they are more apt to move one to sing.[14] That being said, there can be a rejection of the porosity of the "ontological 'yes'" that is not gradually slipped into but instead rapid and deliberate. When Desmond speaks of "covering over"[15] human porosity, he seems to have something more like this in mind. Here various forms of Godlessness could be held responsible, which, in the current milieu of (post-)modernity, tend to come from the same family: that of the *conatus essendi* that has cut its ties with the more primal and life-giving *passio essendi*, thereby affirming the powers of itself alone, so that an "idolatry of autonomy" results.[16] Such a cover-up means that selfhood retreats from what is given to be both from outside of itself and in its innermost, most intimate depths. In the most extreme cases, the desiring self can even reject its own gifted being.

---

12. Desmond, *God and the Between*, 35.

13. Desmond, *God and the Between*, 73.

14. Cf. Desmond, *Philosophy and Its Others*, 269–82; also Desmond, *Being*, 105, 324; and Desmond, *God and the Between*, 76, 122, 197.

15. Desmond, *God and the Between*, 42.

16. Desmond, *God and the Between*, 42.

In each instance, in order that passageways for elemental awareness become open again, a radical transformation must occur, not at the point of the first ontological "yes" (this would be impossible), but instead at those moments of transition, where our hearts must move either toward or away from the goodness of being. It is crucial, again, to emphasize that the possibility to say "yes" rather than "no" is a gift; if this is forgotten, then the whole enterprise is lost, and only an insipid substitute, a counterfeit double[17] to porosity can replace true openness to divine communication intermediated in the *metaxu*. The question then becomes, however, how it is that our pores are to become unclogged at all. Whether slowly blocked or else covered over with the hasty, graceless action characteristic of one anxious to close oneself off to the enigmas of true transcendence and the questions of ultimacy, our pores need to become cleared out, by what Desmond calls a "return to zero."[18] Only in this way can one become truly porous, which is to say, capable of being an emptiness waiting to be filled, transported while at the same time providing passage for divine communication. Such return is a kind of rebirth, preceded by a death to self and confrontation with the realization that all one is and everything in existence are received from agapeic goodness.[19]

Such return can occur in many ways, whether entirely unexpected or else to some degree anticipated. To be porous is, after all, to be open to a variety of modes of infiltration. Something can seep in gradually; or it can overwhelm many pores at once, risking to flood. Means of seepage and freely flowing courses can be identified throughout *God and the Between*, and particularly in discussion of the hyperboles of being. These Desmond describes as "signs in immanence of what transcends immanence and cannot be fully determined in immanent terms."[20] Transcendence, which is "beyond" the between, communicates itself through these signs.[21] To the images of clogging, covering over and unclogging one's pores, Desmond adds another, when speaking of the second hyperbole of being, the *aesthetics of happening*. There he articulates how the hyperbolic can make our pores *sweat*. In this exemplar of porous happening, we become unclogged

---

17. Cf. Desmond, *Hegel's God*, 8–9, and discussion in chapter 2 of the current volume.

18. Cf. especially Desmond, *God and the Between*, 34.

19. I think here especially of Desmond's concept of the "posthumous self," and in particular his reference to this in *God and the Between*, 339–40.

20. Desmond, *God and the Between*, 8.

21. Desmond, *God and the Between*, 8.

and porous, through mediation of the power both within and in excess of us.

According to the aesthetics of happening, the astonishing singularity of things, as they continue to emerge in the ways they have been made, can bring the self to realize the sublimity of being in the between. Desmond reminds us of the milieu of thought from which he speaks, in which modern autonomy blocks our ability to speak about "the glory of creation in its otherness."[22] Such otherness indicates that modern autonomy is insufficient. There is, Desmond argues, a "hyperbolic *in us*," which makes us "sweat," and thus opens us up, both internally and externally. We can reject the hyperbolic, those signs that operate through us and in so-doing transmit the goodness of being. This means insisting on the power of the self, and emphasising the *conatus essendi*. At the same time, such dismissal of otherness denies the possibilities of finding powers within the self, precisely due to a relationship with elemental being. Refusing to see that what is beyond can speak in and through us is a peculiarly modern tendency; on the other hand, denying such closure opens us up to the "sublime"; we can be inspired.[23] Desmond speaks in particular here of artistic inspiration, where technique is transcended by creativity in moments that come from another, yet interior, source.

One should not forget, though, that in order to express her inspiration, the artist needs to have some form of technique in her possession. Inspiration needs another form of perspiration—that of labor, performed so that one can be ready when the hyperbolic takes hold.[24] The hyper-

22. Desmond, *God and the Between*, 136.
23. Desmond, *God and the Between*, 136.
24. Here three of the normal causes of human perspiration may be pertinent. First, there is the sweat involved in learning techniques appropriate for giving form to creativity that seems to arise from within. Here one sweats so as to make way, or prepare, for moments of inspiration. Without her practiced skill, the artist is less able to express hyperbolic revelation in her works of art. Secondly, physical exercise can, through purposeful and sweat-inducing activity, make the person more fit, psychologically and physically, for whatever life might bring. There are spiritual correlates to such exercise, in the traditional religious senses of disciplines, fasts, and regular prayers and sacrifices, each of which both make the person stronger in times of trial, but also prepare them for something more. Athletes of body, mind, and spirit work so as to become attentive to their intermediations in the world. They sweat so as to become open to something more, and so that they can rise to tasks as they present themselves. There is, though, an even more passive way in which one can break out into a sweat, when one is affected by a fever. In this case, the body sweats so as to purge itself of what is unwanted, so as to become healthy again. Such a fever overcomes the one we call the patient, and all one can do is

bolic in us causes us actively to strive, as we receive with a passion that at times we take for granted, while at other moments almost overwhelms with its presence. The striving and willful activity of our *conatus essendi* is a fruitless naught if not infused with creativity that seems almost to come from outside the self, so other can seem the intensity and intimacy of its inwardness. Yet, it is when this passion holds sway—when a fertile "return to zero"[25] has supplanted the urge to become solely self-satisfied—that the truest selving can occur, our erotic desire to become a self delighting in finding itself exceeded by the communication of the agapeic source that constantly calls upward and beyond. As Desmond states in *Art, Origins and Otherness*, "The sweats are not just thought determinations, but the tremors of a shaking in which ontological foundations seem to tremble."[26] In that work, Desmond characterizes the differences between modern and premodern attitudes toward transcendence by identifying their responses to those tremors. Kant, he observes, would arrest his daily walk when the least presentiment of sweat occurred[27], signifying a deep unease with a heteronomy literally expressing itself through the self he wanted to construe as wholly autonomous. Modern *conatus essendi* blacks out the bright resources of the Platonic sun[28] when modern thought approaches anything like the transcendent and hyperbolic.

Desmond's imagery when he speaks of the metaphysical pores of our being strikes a balance between the *conatus essendi* and the *passio essendi*, while asserting the primal importance of our patience to being. We could not strive toward ultimacy were it not for the hyperbolic given within us as well as the cosmos. Our capacity to be astonished and perplexed by the elemental is first bestowed by something beyond. The power of such divine transcendence to arrest us through its intermediations in the *metaxu* is its

---

wait, while the body fights its way back to enjoyment of the elemental again. In these respects, the following observations by Desmond link porosity directly to the *passio essendi* that announces itself in the *sweats*, particularly as athletes describe them. He writes about this elsewhere; see Desmond, "Pluralism, Truthfulness," 65–66. The important thing in all this, he states, is: ". . . to let the flow pass, or begin to pass again, we must get out of our own way, and then we are more truly on the way, and on the way as more truly ourselves."

25. Cf. Desmond, *God and the Between*, 34. This part of *God and the Between* makes it clear that the return to zero is far from a nihilistic nothing. On this point see Desmond, *God and the Between*, 21, 277.

26. Desmond, *Art, Origins*, 232.

27. Desmond, *Art, Origins*, 84.

28. Desmond, *Art, Origins*, 232. For an overview of other modern thinkers in relation to the sweats, see 231–34.

capacity to unclog our pores. This unclogging is most often, according to Desmond's descriptions, gradual, with moments of sudden and heightened awareness of significance. The artist both practicing technique and receiving inspiration is an easily recognizable example. However, the thinker and the religious person are likewise called to labor, so that they can better express intermediations of divine transcendence when intimations from beyond are received. Discussion will now turn to the meaning of *porosity* in Plato's *Symposium*, where Socrates embodies and expresses, through the intermediation of Diotima as well as those around him, the porous, inspired nature of human desire for communication with the divine.

Metaxological Porosity as Socratic *Eros* in Plato's *Symposium*

The significance of the interrelationship between thought and prayer is even more evident in Desmond's philosophy when one explores his derivation of the term *poros* from Plato's *Symposium*. Desmond is especially attentive to the Platonic idea that self-transcending *eros*, when truly mindful, strives to live up to the many elemental ways of the world. The elements are infused with the significance of their source. They are to this extent porous. However, without us that world would not be mindful. It would not be consciously attuned to its source. The hyperbolic within, which gives rise to all forms of being truly mindful, is for Plato present because of the burning Sun, his metaphor for the Good; the *Agathon*, which is our source and ultimate inspiration. Desmond describes the milieu in which we intermediate and are intermediated by the hyperbolic good. He finds that Plato uses the term *metaxu* explicitly in the *Symposium*,[29] to describe *eros*. *Eros*, that is, comes "between" univocity and equivocity. The more, then, we can find about the way that univocity and equivocity are in interplay, the more we can know of our capacities to transcend ourselves, through being "mindful" of their intercommunications.[30]

Desmond finds both of the terms *metaxu* and *poros*[31] in that passage in the *Symposium* where Socrates relates how Diotima in the past has

---

29. Desmond, *God and the Between*, 57, referring to Plato, *Symposium*, 202b5. See also Desmond, *Is There a Sabbath?*, 23–24.

30. Desmond, *God and the Between*, 57.

31. Desmond refers in particular, that is, to Diotima's myth of the origin of *Eros*, whose parents are *Penia* and *Poros*. Cf. Plato, *Symposium*, 203b–c.

questioned his immature assumptions about the nature of *eros*.[32] She convinces the young Socrates of two interrelated points. Firstly, *Eros* is a *daimon*. Neither mortal nor god, he is instead something in between the two, a kind of "glue,"[33] or interconnecting tissue that allows for intercommunications between gods, humans, and the cosmos.[34] *Eros* flies upward and downward, with messages between mortals and divinities, helping humans to pursue their quest for immortality. *Eros* is paradigmatically metaxological, intermediating mortal and divine ways of being and communicating those modes back and forth over what might otherwise be an abyss of dissimilarity and non-communication. Secondly, *Eros* is born of two parents, Resource (*Poros*) and Poverty or Need (*Penia*). Again *Eros* is in between, this time embodying a mediation of what would seem to be the completely disparate features of each parent, and thereby pointing out interrelationships where otherwise there would seem to be none. Rather than completely nullifying either side of the dual parentage expressed in his person, *Eros* expresses something of each at different moments. Certain features of this *daimon*, as described by Diotima speaking through Socrates, remind us very much of the star of the *Symposium*, Socrates[35] himself. In not giving his own account of love, but insisting that he is ignorant about the subject and offering Diotima's views instead, Socrates proves both porous (able to call on a source outside himself and truly capable of hearing what that source tells him, as well as pass on that knowledge) and

---

32. Namely, Plato, *Symposium*, 201d–208d.

33. Cf. Corrigan and Glazov-Corrigan, *Plato's Dialectic*, 120. For a fascinating link, with Augustine here, vis-à-vis "glue," see Burt, *Friendship and Society*, 63.

34. On *eros* as intermediary and in-between, cf. Scott and Welton, *Erotic Wisdom*, 91–92.

35. Cf. Hunter, *Plato's Symposium*, 86: "This mixed being . . . bears a striking resemblance to the normally unshod Socrates, ever 'scheming after the beautiful and the good' . . . while exercising a kind of witchcraft upon others." See also page30, where Hunter sees Socrates' festive garb as his "[physical embodiment of the] literary form of this most festive dialogue, in which philosophy puts on its party face." See also Scott and Welton, *Erotic Wisdom*, 10: whereas all the other speeches have been about *eros*, Alcibiades makes a direct substitution of Socrates for *eros*. See also Scott and Welton, *Erotic Wisdom*, 12–13, where the following points are made to substantiate the claim that Socrates personifies *eros* and the philosophic quest: Diotima's depiction of *eros* resembles Socrates; Socrates claims ignorance about most things, but not about the art of love at 177d–e; and again the structure of the dialogue reinforces the claim (six consecutive speeches on *eros* and then Alcibiades speaks about Socrates).

impoverished (he claims to possess no knowledge entirely his own and so can only repeat what has he has been told).³⁶

Even while enjoying such intermediation between *poros* and *penia*, it is important to note that for Plato and Desmond alike, *poros* is ontologically, if not logically, prior to *penia*.³⁷ Desmond muses that we more often emphasise "*penia* as lack" than we consider the "'resource' of *poros*." This *poros* is one of the philosophical resources for Desmond's "porosity of being."³⁸ He goes on to ask whether being religious entails such porosity, not as a negative (qua lack) but instead a positive resource.³⁹ Such religious resource is to be found in the overdetermination peculiar to porosity, which can be articulated again through Diotima's myth of the conception of *Eros* at the feast of celebration of Aphrodite's birth. There *Penia*, Need personified, begging at the door of the feasting gods, stumbles across a way, given to her by seeming chance, in the personification of *Poros*, fallen drunk and asleep in the garden of Zeus. She lies down beside him, and, in what the ancient Greeks referred to as the rituals of Aphrodite, conceives *Eros*. Need had

---

36. See Sheffield, *Ethics of Desire*, 66: "Socrates divides himself up, so to speak, into two roles—that of the lacking (youthful) Socrates (who is in the same [numbed, ignorant] state as Agathon), and the resourceful Diotima who knows how to remedy the deficiencies in Socrates' *logoi*—we can see his behaviour as embodying the complementarity of these two sides to eros' philosophical nature." Of course, another interpretation is possible here, namely, that Socrates is holding back what he actually knows from those at the party, because he realizes that they would not understand were he to tell them. After all, Socrates seems to be in some ways deliberately donning masks and disguises. He is uncharacteristically dressed up for the party, and at times it is difficult to see if he is being socratically ironic or actually disingenuous. I think in particular of his saccharine-sweet praise of Agathon. On this point of disguise and subterfuge, see Hunter, *Plato's Symposium*, 30, where he reminds us also that Alcibiades warns against taking Socrates's ugly exterior for all there is of him to know. Cf. also Corrigan and Glazov-Corrigan, *Plato's Dialectic*, 37, for Socrates as the one capable of rising above opposites.

37. One formulation of the logical status can be found in Scott and Welton, *Erotic Wisdom*, 101. In Diotima's myth of the origin of *Eros*, there is an important detail, which is that the "principle, that whatever lacks is led to seek what it lacks, is so fundamental that it precedes the birth of *Erôs* in Diotima's theogony, and yet this principle will be embodied in the account of *Erôs* as well." Again this is stated by Sheffield, *Ethics of Desire*, 47: "it is Penia who initiates the interaction with the drunken, stumbling Poros. The experience of a lack is the origin of desire." The ontological point here is that the object of desire would not be desired at all were it not prior and desirable to the subject. In keeping with this is Sheffield's point that *Penia* has at least enough resource to perceive her lack (*Ethics of Desire*, 48).

38. Desmond, *God and the Between*, 41.

39. Desmond, *God and the Between*, 41.

nothing. She was at an aporia.[40] But then she discovered an unexpected gift, a way out of her penury. Because she was willing to beg, she placed herself in a situation to receive. When we become porous, claims Desmond, "we become intimate . . . with . . . gifted poverty," by first "returning to zero."[41] Unclogged porosity makes us as nothing—reminds us that we *are* as nothing in the face of the bounty of all we have been given—and can surprise us with awareness of the power of the "elemental eros of our being,"[42] which is both within and beyond us— intimate, transcendent and universal.

When truly porous we too are beggars at the table of divine abundance.[43] Thereby we become awakened and aroused to the possibilities of gifts already surrounding us. *Poros* lies asleep when found by *Penia*. As Kevin Corrigan and Elena Glazov-Corrigan observe: "Clearly, Plenty's [*Poros*'s] sleep betokens something like pure divine superabundance, as expressive of both its inner festive nature and its consequences; and this divine superabundance provides the occasion for generation of a different kind of reality [*Eros*]."[44] In Plato's myth, the *eros* that we experience, the urgency of our quest for selving and for transcendence, is, when personified, the means by which the gods become aware of who and what we are. *Eros* carries our petitions to the gods. At the same time, *Eros* brings messages of the divine life, which would otherwise have no way to be known and felt. The *Symposium* may not speak of *agape*, but elements of this superabundant and overdetermined love described by Desmond are not entirely lacking in the dialogue.[45] Socrates lives out some of the most significant of

---

40. Cf. Sheffield, *Ethics of Desire*, 58: "Poros is linked to *euporia* . . . linguistically and conceptually . . . and Penia is likewise connected with *aporia*." And "Socrates himself was notorious for being in a state of aporia, and for putting others in a similar state too" (60).

41. Desmond, *God and the Between*, 41.

42. Desmond, *God and the Between*, 41.

43. Scott and Welton, *Erotic Wisdom*, 92: "Diotima's teaching suggests that somehow *all* desires are connected to the divine, although some are connected more and others less directly. All desires have some relation to the divine, but some desires are closer to the divine than others."

44. Corrigan and Glazov-Corrigan, *Plato's Dialectic*, 126.

45. Cf. Scott and Welton, *Erotic Wisdom*, 11: "The Greek word, *Erôs*, means love as passionate desire, especially sexual desire; but as the dialogue progresses the meaning of *Erôs* can range from homoerotic sexual desire to a cosmic force of attraction binding the elements of nature into a harmonious whole, and from such 'cosmic love' to the fundamental longing humans have for all the kinds of things they lack." Also page 25: "Plato's vision of Philosophy as love is unique in the history of Philosophy. In the

these, in the drama of the dialogue and extending beyond it. Socrates lost in thought at the beginning of the *Symposium*,[46] as he often is according to Alcibiades later in the dialogue,[47] is a portrait of the one who attends to what is given, giving himself over to thought, and waiting and seizing upon those moments when thought gives something to him that is describable in its unexpected givenness as transcendent. If, as others in the dialogue declare, Socrates can hold himself back from the Dionysian effects of alcohol and from the physical urges of simple eroticism, he is also able to give himself over, succumbing to a need that is not purely negative, but instead the opening of a way. Again, *poros* is summoned in its ontological priority: Socrates entranced in thought is involved in intimate appreciation of what it is to undergo the presence of transcendent otherness.[48] The

---

Symposium, he goes beyond the etymology of the word "philosophy," to suggest that philosophy is not merely a philia (friend or friendship) of wisdom, but nothing less than an *Erôs*, an insatiable hunger for wisdom *that is never finally possessed*" (italics original). They also indicate the religious aspect held in common to all Diotima's forms of *eros*: "Diotima's teaching contains the beginnings of a Philosophy of Religion . . . suggest[ing] that somehow *all* desires are connected to the divine, although some are connected more and others less directly" (92). On the cosmic link, bringing together mortal and divine, see 95–96. Also cf. Bury, *Symposium of Plato*, xlviii, who refers to Jowett's commentary, saying: "this blend [in *eros* described by Diotima] of passion and reason is accompanied by the further qualification of religious emotion and awe." Bury relates Diotima's account to the psalmist's "thirst for God" and clarifies: "This change of atmosphere results from the new vision of the goal of Eros, no longer identified with any earthly object, but with the celestial and divine Idea . . . Thus the pursuit of Beauty becomes in the truest sense a religious exercise, the efforts spent on Beauty become genuine devotions, and the honours paid to Beauty veritable oblations" (xlix). Compare the Platonic notion of *eros* set forth in the *Symposium* with that purportedly more common in Plato's time, as described, for instance, in Dover, "Introduction," 44ff. Dover defines *eros* as "any very strong desire (e.g. for victory) and is used also by Homer . . . to denote appetite for food and drink, usually means 'love' in the sense which that word bears in our expression 'be in love (with . . .)' . . . and 'fall in love (with . . .)' . . . : that is, intense desire for a particular individual as a sexual partner" (1); and "The Greeks generally agreed . . . in treating the difference between eros and ordinary sexual desire as quantitative (Prodicus . . . defined eros as 'desire doubled,' adding that 'eros doubled' is 'madness') and in treating both as essentially a response to the stimulus afforded by the sight of a person who is καλός" (2). For comparisons and contrasts between *eros* and *philia*, see also Corrigan and Glazov-Corrigan, *Plato's Dialectic*, 44ff.

46. Cf. Plato, *Symposium*, 174d–175d.
47. Cf. Plato, *Symposium*, 220c–d.
48. Cf. Scott and Welton, *Erotic Wisdom*, 35: "Socrates' remarks about the evanescent character of his 'wisdom' and Socrates' trance on the porch may be hints of the paradoxical character of the philosopher's simultaneous communion with and distance from the divinity he seeks." There seems more to this trance than the simple dualistic explanation

unaided incommunicability to others—at least, the company he is with in this particular dialog—of such a communication points to something fundamental about porosity. Socrates may be afraid to attempt an exposition of the nature of love based on his experience alone, but he is willing to call upon the voice of another. That Socrates repeats what Diotima tells him signifies that readiness. In a more acute sense, he seems aware that in prayer and the most sublime forms of thought, to be open to mediation from beyond requires being overcome and thus surrendering the pretence that one's interior life is completely one's own. That is, as Augustine might well say, it is to acknowledge that there is something more intimate to me than anything I might know of myself.

If we think of Socrates' vision as a kind of prayer, then his well-considered speech and actions can be directly related to Desmond's understanding of porosity. The primal porosity that allows one to be religious and philosophical alike begins in prayer that overwhelms before it can be spoken. And the speech that it instigates may not at first be possible in simple words, but only in the interstices—which is to say, the pores—that mediate as direct communication as there can be between divine and human. Love forms this mediating space within Socrates' speech. It is the making of a way that is overdetermined before it can be traversed. When we love what is given to us, our existence forms various places for the goodness of being to announce itself within the world. It is there, in-between, that the truest forms of thought and prayer unify poverty and resource, by acknowledging that they proceed from an overdetermined, primal porosity of being. When the terms of *penia* and *poros* are translated into the language of Saint Augustine, they achieve even further religious resonance. It is to this way of speaking that the present discussion of porosity will now turn.

Desire's Porous Mediation in Augustine's Theology of Prayer

From its origins in thought in the milieu of the *Symposium*, one can see that porosity is inseparable from the movement of *eros*. However, as Augustine

---

given by, among others, R. G. Bury. See for instance Bury, *Symposium of Plato*, xix. There he says it is an illustration of the "entire subordination of flesh to spirit in which Socrates was unique." Socrates may not seem to the outsider as though physically transported. However, *eros*, personified by Socrates, seems to give new meaning to the flesh, rather than denying it completely.

says even more explicitly than Plato (at least in that dialog), such porosity is only possible when love is properly directed. Augustine may not employ the term *porosity*, but it is clear that for him, prayer makes us increasingly porous to the ways of divine beneficence. That is, through prayer's intermediation we become existentially open to divine communication, and more apt to recognise the latter through the working words of prayer. As Desmond's imagery reminds, the pores of our being can only transmit what God would tell us through the *metaxu* when they have been unclogged and cleared out. In the *Symposium*, the lover of ultimacy motivates his or her erotic striving for philosophical truth with a healthy acknowledgement of ignorance in the face of the overdetermined value of being. For Augustine, our movement toward restlessness, lived and expressed in prayer, involves the acknowledgement that without God we are nothing. Prayer proves the presence and increases the intensity of our divinely bestowed and directed love. Furthermore, when prayer takes the form of words, it also allows us to perform a check on how intimately we experience that love's presence. This, another expression of our "return to zero," brings the self before itself in the presence of God. In the most intense forms of prayer, one acknowledges that God is more intimate to me than I am to myself. This realization entails that God precedes me at the very core of selfhood, so that I am as nothing and a beggar even for knowledge of my desiring self.

I will now articulate several of Augustine's insights into the nature of prayer, particularly as prayer relates to the work of thought, so as to elucidate further the importance of ontological porosity in Desmond's metaxological metaphysics. The first point involves Augustine's emphasis on the role of love in the world and in our relationship to God and its relation to the same for Plato and for Desmond. Secondly, we see how for Augustine thought and prayer work together to orient our love properly. Finally, the nature and source of our interior intimacy with God is illuminated according to its ultimate ground. Desmond often echoes two of Augustine's maxims: that God is more intimate to me than I am to myself; and that our movement in the world toward God proceeds from exterior to interior and inferior to superior. Both of these can be understood, in Desmond's and, of course, Augustine's views of our ontological openness to love, by seeing that Augustine, like Plato, holds that humans have a gifted and simultaneously beggarly relationship to divine bestowals.

This discussion seeks not to point out Platonic influences on Augustine but rather Platonic and Augustinian resonances in Desmond's thought with regard to religious porosity. That being said, there are of course strong similarities between Plato's and Augustine's understanding of the role and nature of love in the human quest for happiness in the presence of the divine. For each, the love that motivates us in everything we do has a divine source. Our lives are for both philosophers ultimately religiously oriented, as each of us seeks the fitting end to restless desire in coming to know and experience the presence of divine transcendence. While they use different terms to speak about the nature of love both Plato and Augustine emphasise its religious tenor. As Scott and Welton point out, the religious character of *eros* for Plato is precisely such that "Humans desire the gifts of the gods, and somehow, through this very desire, are guided by the gods. The object of desire has an impact on the psyche."[49] In other words, it has a transformative impact on the person. For Augustine, this is even more explicitly the case. *Amor* drives everything that exists, and especially the human quest for meaning and intimate relationship to God.[50] However, what we love defines, changes, and motivates us in everything we do. When we love with *caritas*, we are close to the divine source. When we love only with *cupiditas*, we use what is in the world, taking it for granted without crediting its source. We impose designs upon it, with what Desmond would call the spirit of *conatus essendi*.

As Desmond therefore contends, our porosity involves living a "return to zero" wherever possible, so as to remain alert to the importance of the *passio essendi* in our quest for knowledge of the intermediations of transcendence. This is how we come to know *eros* as the mediating point of divine communication. It should be remembered, though, that within Desmond's thought *eros* alone is not enough. The love that Desmond names agapeic is hinted at by Plato. After all, within the *Symposium*, goodness and beauty are the ultimate and transcendent end toward which *eros* strives; and *penia*, a vacuum of all that she needs to survive, finds *poros* unexpectedly there

---

49. Scott and Welton, *Erotic Wisdom*, 93.

50. For an extended discussion of the role of love in Augustine's thought, see Arendt, *Love and Saint Augustine*. See also Jackson, "Faith, Hope, and Charity." Compare also with Scott and Welton's reading of Plato (*Erotic Wisdom*, 94): "No matter what the object of one's love, love informs one's life"; see also 105–6. Desire is, furthermore, a participation in the good: "the very desire for the Good contains a message and an inspiration from the Good, i.e., the Good's nature is communicated to humans to an extent through their desire for it . . . This connection between the Divine and mortal objects of desire provides an incentive to care about another's good and to identify another's good)or the other's progress toward the good) with one's own. Diotima's view of *Erôs* is no more deficient than any *religious* view of love." Scott and Welton, *Erotic Wisdom*, 150.

and able to fulfill her lack.⁵¹ Even when it seems arbitrary and impersonal, Platonic *eros* can never be fully separated from the reach of divine love. Desmond's sense of *eros* goes beyond and into the realm of *agape*, showing its possibilities for intimately personal communications of divine transcendence. For Desmond, the thoughts and prayers which emerge from *eros* oriented toward the divine become religious inasmuch as they arise from but also nourish an interior relationship to what is absolute. This sense of divine intimacy, known through the interior workings of love, may not be found so precisely within Plato's account, but it is present in Augustine's thought. We now turn to the Augustinian aspects of porosity religiously and philosophically considered in *God and the Between*, by exploring Augustine's appreciation of the relation between the defining character of prayer and its related spoken thoughts of prayer.

For Augustine, it is evident that prayer is not essentially an account of what we would like to have from God, but instead a communication with him, so as to attune the self to what God has given and wants from us. As Henry Chadwick observes, for Augustine, "in prayer we use words but well know that they do not inform God of anything he does not know or can conceivably have forgotten."⁵² Through prayer, desire becomes oriented toward its truest object.⁵³ Thereby, we come to know that we are nothing

---

51. In this respect too, it is interesting to note that the last word of the *Symposium* is the Greek for "respite" or "rest" (cf. Corrigan and Glazov Corrigan, *Plato's Dialectic*, 38). The authors make of this that the horizontal dimensions of desire (what I would add in the *Republic* Socrates speaks of as the domain of mixed desires) comes together with the vertical, religious dimension in the person of Socrates. Socrates, unlike the others, can stay up all night talking and then go about his daily business before taking rest. I would take further from this a sense of interior peace in Socrates that bespeaks Desmond's *agapeic*, attuned to the nourishment a Sabbath provides, and Augustine's divinely directed *caritas*, which marks the end to restless love. Another aspect of *agape* perhaps present in Plato's *eros* might be that of a "two-way friendship" between the gods and men. Cf. Corrigan and Glazov-Corrigan, *Plato's Dialectic*, 121: this is "opposed to the common scholarly view, for eg., that in Plato's thought we love the gods, but the gods don't love us back . . . It seems a reasonable inference at this point that while we could hardly suppose divine 'love' to be like human 'love,' since Eros is a spirit and not a god, nonetheless friendship and love in some sense must also mark the gods' relation to humankind . . . a new theology is suggested, so close to traditional accounts in some ways and yet with a new emphasis on the dialogical relationship of Love between the divine and human worlds. This may help to explain for a modern reader the peculiar enthusiasm of all later antiquity for the story that is to follow [about the origin of *Eros*]."

52. Chadwick, *Augustine of Hippo*, 46.

53. For discussion of this and many of the other main points of Augustinian prayer see the richly annotated Hand, *Saint Augustine on Prayer*.

without God, and that only through and with him is any fulfilment of desire attainable. This picture of the possibilities for human love must remain to hand when approaching Augustine's appreciation of the nature and role of prayer in our lives.

In his "Letter 130," Augustine brings together many of his most significant points about the nature of prayer.[54] There he states that: "God does not want our will, which he cannot fail to know, to become known to him, but our desire, by which we can receive what he prepares to give, to be exercised in prayers."[55] In other words, the purpose of prayer is not to tell God what he already knows, about what we want.[56] God instead desires that we pray so that we can desire what he constantly gives. In so-doing, we give what is most intimate back to him who gave it to us first. In fact, we could not desire at all, which means that we could not pray, were it not for God's grace: true prayer is always on God's terms and with the aid of his love. One can think here of Augustine's observation, a moment before his conversion, that he willed to turn to God, but could not, because his desire was not yet properly directed.[57] Not until God had transformed him could he conform,[58] in keeping with a divine transformation at the core of his being, which would thenceforth reverberate through all he would do and say. Similarly, Desmond observes in *God and the Between* that humans cannot pray by calling on a simple will to pray. Prayer is, instead, both "the highest form of listening speech" and at the same time "speechless."[59] It is a "possibility" that cannot happen due to human powers alone.[60] "We can will to pray, but that will does not constitute prayer."[61] With the moment of enacting prayer comes the realization that prayer moves through us, in a communication that is more divine than human. It is as if the platonic *daimon* of *eros* takes up residence within, making of the human heart a space of *passio essendi*. Porous, one becomes an empty chasm where *eros* is

54. Augustine, *Letters 100–155*, 183–99.

55. Augustine, *Letters 100–155*, 130.17.

56. For the essential division between *oratio* and *laus* in Augustine's terminology concerning prayer, and some of the main points about prayer per se in his thought, see Weaver, "Prayer."

57. See Augustine, *Confessions*, 8.19–25.

58. Timothy Maschke speaks of this dynamic of what he calls "gracious conformation" (Maschke, "St. Augustine's Theology of Prayer").

59. Desmond, *God and the Between*, 195.

60. Desmond, *God and the Between*, 195.

61. Desmond, *God and the Between*, 195.

not a messenger to distant divinities. Instead, God announces his interior presence, and with that an intimacy more profound than any which one could ever determinately iterate.

Accordingly, for Augustine and Desmond alike, prayer is not characterized by the mere composition and utterance of words. Augustine explicitly states that words are not even necessary for prayer to occur. Desire, rather than speech, is vital. Augustine explains that St. Paul's admonishment that one should "pray without ceasing" does not mean the constant use of "many words," for "[m]uch talking is one thing; a lasting love is another."[62] There are many ways of prayer, and for Augustine prayers that use words hold an ancillary function to the proper work of communication, through desire, with the one who gives all. For him, prayer has to do with the "long and pious stirring of the heart," a

> task . . . very often carried out more with sighs than words, more with weeping than with speaking. But [God] places our tears in his sight, and our sighing is not hidden from him who created all things by his Word and does not seek human words.[63]

Again, desire is the engine of prayer, and its truer expressions come through more elemental forms of communication than the work of speech. As Desmond observes, song can be more in keeping with the language of prayer than the simple spoken word. Prayer's elemental nature naturally couples with music, which at its best moves through the musician while proceeding from the core of his or her being.[64]

Nonetheless, in Augustine's theory there is porosity between thought and prayer, such that our active employment of words to express our desire can both fine-tune and at the same time present to us in thought the condition of our relationship to God. That is, firstly, we can with careful consideration attune ourselves properly to what God wants us to be, by praying with the words that Christ explicitly gave us, in the Lord's Prayer. There, praise comes first, followed by petitions for those things that we can justly desire in our quest toward his life of grace and happiness, here and ultimately in eternity. This, the "happy life," is that for which we aim—the life, that is, of

---

62. Augustine, *Letters 100–155*, 130.18. Similarly he says in sermon 56: ". . . when you pray, it's devotedness you need, not wordiness." Not to put too fine a point on it, he continues: ". . . the reason he wanted you to pray is so that he can give to an eager recipient, not to one who is bored with what he has given." Augustine, *Sermons 51–94*, 56.4.

63. Augustine, *Letters 100–155*, 130.20.

64. Cf. Desmond, *God and the Between*, 134.

eternal beatitude in the presence of God and the communion of angels and saints.[65] Secondly though, words recall us to ourselves. Augustine explains, again speaking of our need to "pray without ceasing," that we should

> always desire [the happy life] and always pray for this from the Lord God. But at certain hours, by the words of prayer, we call the mind back to the task of praying from other cares and concerns, which in a sense cool down this desire.[66]

Through the words of prayer, then, our requests are placed in their right context, so that they "become known to us before God through our patience."[67] This patience, like the *passio essendi* of which Desmond speaks, is the most vital aspect of our relationship to God, because it expresses, as it were, our ontological status in relationship to him. Nothing, not even what we want, is ours alone, because all has been given to us.

Desmond seeks this same ontological structure of the human heart by tracing the Augustinian route of desire toward God, from exterior to interior and from inferior to superior. Through the hyperboles of being, we find within ourselves the power, given from elsewhere, to intermediate divine presence in and through the world. Thus, what would seem to be purely external, the cosmos in its many dimensions, is elementally present, unified with elemental experience and appreciation. Our thoughts, as expressions of that mediation, ring true with such hyperbolic reach and range when they proceed from prayer, or, as Desmond describes, when they are "surprised" by prayer.[68] At such moments, thought and prayer become so porous to each other, so genuinely gifted, as to become almost indistinguishable. In evidently issuing from the desiring self, while yet coming from a source elsewhere, philosophy and prayer reveal the intimacy of their source. By being more intimate to the self than it is to itself, God reveals

---

65. In aiming for that goal, both praise and petition have their roles in prayer. What is crucial is that they retain the same overall orientation as in the Lord's Prayer. Cf. Jackson, "Lord's Prayer." See also Augustine's "Exposition 2 of Psalm 26," which emphasizes that in this life we experience anxiety and so it is proper that we pray, realizing that our prayer will turn from groaning and praise into only praise (Augustine, *Expositions of the Psalms 1–32*, 26.2.14. See also "Exposition of Psalm 104," where Augustine emphasizes that praise precedes petition and also that our desire for God and search for him never ends. That is, even in the presence of the beloved (eternally in the case of life with God in heaven) desire does not cease (Augustine, *Expositions of the Psalms 99–120*, 104.184–87).

66. Augustine, *Letters 100–155*, 130.18.

67. Augustine, *Letters 100–155*, 130.18.

68. Desmond, *God and the Between*, 45.

himself through the most personal and interior sources of the erotic desire to selve. *Agape* precedes *eros* as the primal porosity out of which thought and prayer both proceed, as they intertwine and move toward the point of that same agapeic origination of all.

First and Last Porous Returns to Zero

Desmond describes *poros* as "the making of a way," as a "transition that is no transition," which withdraws in order to open up the way.[69] This tension of giving way so as to receive is impossible without the divine gift of allowing the self to become as nothing, reveling in the *passio essendi*. When the din of *eros* aimed only at self determining goals quietens, *conatus essendi* no longer has the upper hand. Plato and Augustine express this same insight; for them, our relationship to divine transcendence is like that of a beggar. For Plato, we cannot receive the energy vital to thought without embodying *penia*'s sense of need as well as *poros*'s resource. Socrates lives this dynamic on a daily basis. Augustine speaks directly to the same point, reminding that in prayer we do well to remember that we are impoverished and at the same time the receivers of everything that we have, including the gift of prayer. Warning against holding that prayer comes from the self alone, Augustine interrogates his congregation with the words, "Beggar man . . . what, after all, have you got that you have not received? . . . your indigence and beggary, unless [God] had first given you something, would have remained a total void."[70] In order to become this fruitful empty space, he argues, we must practice "a certain learned ignorance."[71] Like socratic ignorance, this is related to Desmond's "return to zero," which is necessary to strike a balance between *passio essendi* and *conatus essendi*, so as to allow for more and greater paths of porosity to run through us. We are not completely inactive when waiting for divine inspiration. Unclogged porosity demands precisely that we practice an attitude that already marks out some of the pathways through which divine communications might then traverse.

---

69. Desmond, *God and the Between*, 41.

70. Augustine, *Sermons 148–183*, 168.4. See also sermon 56, where Augustine speaks of the Lord's Prayer, saying: "When you say, *Give us this day our daily bread*, you are admitting that you are begging from God. But don't be ashamed about it; however rich anyone may be on earth, he has to beg from God" (Augustine, *Sermons 51–94*, 56.9).

71. Augustine, *Letters 100–155*, 130.28.

Desmond's call for porosity between thought and prayer, religion and philosophy, derives from his understanding of how our ontological porosity announces itself in everyday life. In *God and the Between*, the ways in which the transcendent source makes known its presence in things great and small are striking in their quotidian availability. The reader becomes aware that porosity demands elemental attentiveness on our part. Desmond describes:

> The call of this life is to live the holy in the good of being, vigilant to the hyperboles of the agapeic that in immanent life communicate of divine transcendence. Most of these communications are godsends that come quietly. The agapeics of the divine arrive unobtrusively in the most hidden of elemental things: a mustard seed, a smile, a song, a glint of sun, a drink of pure water, a child holding one's hand, the comfort of fire on a bitter day, the uninsistent aid of an agapeic servant. The agapeics of the good communicate almost nothing and yet without them life loses its charge of worthiness, becoming loveless and unloved.[72]

The very stillness with which such intimations of divinely bestowed worth come into our lives already presents a challenge to what might become clogged porosity. The beauty and goodness[73] of these elemental intermediations can be overlooked if one constantly insists that without the self they would be meaningless. By attending to the "almost nothing" of the elemental, we can imitate its porous paths.

Instead of insisting only on the self then, one is called to realize that elemental communications proceed from a worthy whole that exists regardless of one's desires or determinations. In Desmond's terminology, human life then becomes "permeable" to prayer as a "communication" with God.[74] Such prayer, he says, is mostly intermittent.[75] However, as we have seen from Augustine's understanding of prayer, this very irregularity is essential to the ways along which we ceaselessly pray. Translated into metaxological terms, when one lives out one's porosity elementally, *eros* runs together with the agapeic mediations that make prayer possible. Such prayer can

---

72. Desmond, *God and the Between*, 338.

73. While this study has not directly touched on this point, it should not be forgotten that beauty and goodness hold an ambiguous relationship to each other in the *Symposium*, sometimes seeming to be identical and at other times distinct. See Hunter, *Plato's Symposium*, 87; Scott and Welton, *Erotic Wisdom*, 107.

74. Desmond, *God and the Between*, 338.

75. Desmond, *God and the Between*, 338.

happen at regular intervals only when we are open to the gifted moments of heightened awareness of agapeic goodness that are equally a kind of prayer.

Such attunement is possible only when we nurture the "return to zero" critical to fertile reception of communications of divine transcendence. As Desmond points out, in keeping with his Platonic and Augustinian roots, the erotics of selving, when open to agapeic communication, opens us up, making us porous to what is other and beyond. Thus we can transcend ourselves because we are porous, and such porosity depends upon a primal openness to "transcendence as other" and at the same time beyond the self.[76] This is the paradox of porosity: we find ourselves by first surrendering to that which lies beyond. Returning to zero is crucial to such opening and constitutes our openness, our porosity. Our return occurs not only once but instead constitutes moment upon moment of "ontological 'yes,'" allows us to be "shaken to the elements," and receptive to the power of prayer. This is comparable to the practiced ignorance that both Socrates and Augustine recommend. Acknowledging that essentially one knows nothing that is not hyperbolically given from both within and beyond is the labor prior to moments of complete unclogging and simultaneous opening of one's pores. Not only does Socrates practice ignorance, but he brings others into that state, breaking down the *conatus essendi* to make way for the truest forms of knowledge, which cannot come from the self alone.[77] As Socrates demonstrates in the *Symposium* and elsewhere, in order to know, the philosopher must first admit not knowing. Only then can he or she receive the riches of thought, which meld into semblance of prayer. Similarly, Augustine ultimately argues that our "learned ignorance" entails that we should pray that all our requests and desires be fulfilled in the ultimate eternal peace that we know we cannot fully appreciate here and now. The greater our awareness of this lack of existentially significant knowledge, the more intimate and intense will be our prayer.

All of this means that we are true to the overdetermined nature of the *metaxu* when thought proves porous to prayer and vice versa, because each is open to the transmission of agapeic goodness. This goodness is, in

---

76. Desmond, *God and the Between*, 12.

77. Scott and Welton suggest that Socrates' love, the art of which has been taught to him by Diotima, is that which makes him who and what he is. He numbs and confuses through questioning, thus awakening desire for knowledge like his own desire: "This awakening of love could be part of the erotic art that Socrates claims is the only thing he understands" (Scott and Welton, *Erotic Wisdom*, 88). Also: it is a "positive kind of ignorance" (25).

Augustine's terms, the proper and ultimate end to our restless longing. It comprises a peace so great in its intensity that we cannot yet really know it. Augustine elaborates: ". . . this is peace that surpasses all understanding, even when we ask for it in prayer, *we do not know what we should pray for as we ought. For we, of course, do not know what we cannot think of as it is.*"[78] Thought is porous to prayer—as a way through which prayer can pass—when it goes as far as it can in thinking what it knows it cannot ever know without the grace of God's final revelation. It should not be forgotten, though, that prayer is also porous to something more. Prayer, as Desmond calls it, is a "bestowed, gifted energy."[79] Such vitality is elemental, running through us and reaching upwards to its superior source. Like Socrates, we should be open to seeking it wherever we can, opening others to its ways, and stopping in our tracks to revel in its presence whenever we have the opportunity to do so.

For Desmond, Plato and Socrates, and Augustine, thought and prayer alike depend on divine gracious giving in order to exist. Moreover, thought and prayer can become so porous to each other as to be almost indistinguishable. That is, thought and prayer that communicate with our ontological foundations are defined by their extraordinary acceptance of their impoverishment metaphysically prior to the offerings of divine transcendence. Being porous means never losing that sense of being beggars. Thought and prayer need to ask in order to receive the truths imparted through their interstices.

Finally, porosity reveals that the *passio essendi* is far from passive complacency. It is passion in active, desiring anticipation of a new birth of self that reveals our former selfhood to have been as yet "unborn."[80] Thought and prayer, constantly given to us, are the modes in which we exercise our hope of being transported and transformed by elementally, hyperbolically configured divine communications in the *metaxu*. The unclogging of porosity is a continual task that it is not ours alone to undertake. Its learned ignorance is a submergence into a kind of nothing,[81] so as to emerge and pass by turns through elementally configured thought and prayer, moving toward erotic determinations of self that are possible only because of the constant agapeic presence of the divinely bestowed *metaxu*.

78. Augustine, *Letters 100–155*, 130.26 (italics original).
79. Desmond, *God and the Between*, 202.
80. Cf. Desmond, *God and the Between*, 337–38.
81. Cf. Desmond, *God and the Between*, 340.

4

Thinking Transcendence, Transgressing the Mask

Desmond Pondering Augustine and Thomas Aquinas

AUGUSTINE AND AQUINAS HAVE been Desmond's companions for some time now. Frequent quotations from Augustine, together with adoption of that saint's movement from the exterior to the interior and the inferior to the superior make that particular friendship quite evident.[1] Aquinas is less frequently referred to, but in *The Intimate Strangeness of Being* Desmond describes the more systematic writer as "one of those thinkers for me whom I would call *companioning*. Such a thinker one does not necessarily make into an object of scholarly research, but yet he forms a presence as a companion."[2] This exploration will not assume that it is only because Augustine and Aquinas are both theologians as well as philosophers that they can aid to know how Desmond offers something to theology. Instead, it will go to one of their shared insights concerning transcendence, to demonstrate how Desmond, in agreeing with them, vivifies an ancient intuition:

---

1. See for instance the epigraph to *God and the Between*, taken from Augustine's *Confessions*: *Sacrificem tibi famulatum cogitationis et linguae meae, et da quod offeram tibi.* The present volume strives to explore the various ways in which Desmond communicates with Augustine as a companion in thought. Another specific place in which Desmond is explicit about his relationship to Augustine is in "St. Augustine's *Confessions.*"

2. Desmond, *Intimate Strangeness*, 232. Chapter 9 of that work, entitled "Analogy, Dialectic, and Divine Transcendence: Between St. Thomas and Hegel" (231–59), is the third in what Desmond calls a "triad" of essays about Thomas. The other two in the triad are Desmond, *Is There a Sabbath?*, chapter 10 ("Is there a Sabbath for Thought: Reflections of Philosophy and Peace," 312–56; and Desmond, "Exceeding Virtue."

that through adopting a mask, the human person can mediate and be mediated by the created world. This is only possible when one acknowledges that one is "nothing" in face of the "more" of God.

I will endeavour to explore these points in the following way. First, I will speak of masking and doubling in Desmond's philosophy. Then I will consider Augustine and Thomas in turn, in the ways that they use masks. Finally I will discuss how analogy is an appropriate way of speaking of God for all three speakers, before considering how Augustine, Aquinas and Desmond are all thinkers of ontological peace. My exploration of Thomas will be more extended than of Augustine in this chapter, so as to supplement and draw out what is argued in the other chapters of this book.

The Meaning of the Mask: Personal Enactment of Doubling

Desmond's idea of the mask relies on his notion of doubling, and forms a way for him to counteract the "counterfeit double" of Hegel's God.[3] Essentially, for Desmond, Augustine and Thomas succeed in adopting masks for themselves, while recognizing and expressing God's masks, because they know that a mask at its best exceeds determinate rational speculation and offers a way to know what is "more." Neither thinker explores and articulates a "counterfeit double" of God, but appreciates instead that God is always beyond what can be thought and stated. For Desmond, Aquinas's understanding of plurivocity, inspired by Aristotle's *Metaphysics* as well as by Augustine's appreciation of the way that God speaks through his creation, has "metaphysical dimensions." Namely, "the plurivocity is of being itself, and not simply our ways of talking about it. Our ways of speaking it are to be true to being's way(s) of bespeaking itself—plurivocally."[4] Thinking about the mask enables one to know how a person can enter into the mystery of such plurivocity, because a mask enables the philosopher to speak about transcendence without thereby opting only for the univocal, equivocal or dialectical. Thomas's analogical predication is blood-brother to Desmond's metaxological voicing.

---

3. On this point, it is helpful to consider some of Desmond's remarks on the need for images for thought, and when these can turn counterfeit, in particular in Desmond, *Hegel's God*, 8–9. For the connection between person and double, see also Desmond, *Ethics*, 190–91.

4. Desmond, *Intimate Strangeness*, 234.

Such speech depends upon the personal nature of philosophical enquiry, which in turn relies upon the capacity to work with masks that both represent and point beyond what can be said. In *God and the Between*, Desmond makes this link by explaining the mask in direct relationship to the "plurivocal manifestation" of being. The mask, says Desmond, has its origins in late Roman times, as *persona* or *prosopon*. Desmond will find *persona* more compelling as a way to think of the mask than *prosopon*, because the latter refers more to optics, whereas *persona* connotes sound, and thus the way that divine speech can sound through us, if we are porous to that possibility.[5] In any case, donning the *persona*, the actor became a nexus of doubleness, enabling the double mediation that Desmond speaks of elsewhere as both "self-mediation (thought thinking itself in thinking its other) and intermediation (thought thinking its other)."[6] In other words, doubleness emphasises that self-reflection is only possible through the other; and at the same time that otherness is not reducible to that mode of self-reflection. Self and other remain in fertile tension, and can mediate each other either detrimentally or effectively.

When dialectical, this mediation becomes self-focused and self-enclosed, because the other is used only as a means for the self; rather than left to be in its otherness, while at the same time also being a resource for the self. Masking as metaxological mediation works in the following ways. When someone dons a mask, particularly on stage, she represents something else while remaining herself, thus allowing something to be seen because of her disguise. Furthermore, the mask acts as a medium through which otherwise unrealizable possibilities of the human person can unfold. The mask enables intermediation, between self, world and others. Desmond describes this in *God and the Between*: the mask opens up a "passage" between the *persona* that the actor adopts and the performance as it is seen.[7] Something is always held back, or operates in excess, of such enactment, so that the character known through the mask both reveals and conceals. The audience can see something, but not all of the character, through the operation of the mask.[8] Thus, the self is fully there, but represented as holding back something of itself. What is reserved is in this case openly represented

---

5. Desmond, *God and the Between*, 192. Chapter 9 in that work contains references to the "more" and the "nothing" discussed in the present chapter.
6. See Simpson, *Religion, Metaphysics*, 32.
7. Desmond, *God and the Between*, 192.
8. Desmond, *God and the Between*, 192.

Thinking Transcendence, Transgressing the Mask

within the context of performance: the masked self undergoes a particular enactment that is of the self and yet other to the self; the self represents something that it is and yet is not.

This understanding of personhood, known *through* the mask, relies on the notion of porosity, which Desmond finds key for approaching God in any way adequately.[9] Only through allowing oneself to become as nothing can God in his otherness announce and be heard. Thereby, one becomes a passage through which transcendence speaks—a per-sonans rather than a pros-opon, which is to say a person understood as "an acoustic passage," a porous channel through which the divine other comes into the world through words or song.[10] Thus can thought truly sing its other.[11]

Personal porosity, thought through the doubleness of the mask, has extraordinary implications when coupled with the notions of "more" and "nothing" that Desmond uncovers in the thought of both Augustine and Thomas Aquinas. For let us consider another way in which Desmond thinks the implications of the mask, as a device that allows discovery of what is in the self precisely through offering the pretense that one is otherwise than the self. Desmond thinks here of Prince Hamlet's taking on of mania, which almost turns upon to take him over entirely. The mask can be deceptive, negatively pointing toward the fact that the inner person can never be completely revealed.[12] The mask makes evident an otherness to the self that is at the same time of the self. Even when one takes on a mask, one is never in complete control, but instead at risk of revealing through adopting that particular mask some aspect of the very thing that one wants to hide. Kierkegaard is a case in point. Each pseudonym allows another posture of thought, so that his fervor constantly emerges, and with it a wail against systematization of the divine. Just as Pascal cannot forgive Descartes, Desmond notes that Kierkegaard cannot absolve Hegel for reducing God to a dialectician's mask: a facade with nothing beyond or behind.[13]

Tellingly, when crossing swords with Hegel, Desmond does not call upon Kierkegaard as his boon companion so much as he does Augustine

---

9. See for instance Desmond, *God and the Between*, 284, where porosity is important for us to become a "kind of nothing" capable of prayer. See also Desmond, *Intimate Strangeness*, 21–25.

10. Desmond, *God and the Between*, 197

11. See in particular Desmond, *Philosophy, Others*, chapter 6: "Being Mindful: Thought Singing Its Other" (259–311).

12 Desmond, *Philosophy, Others*, 78.

13. Desmond, *Beyond Hegel*, 156–60.

and Aquinas. The mask he adopts, like a shield, to address Hegel's "counterfeit double" takes elements of the more porous masks of Augustine, particularly in his *Confessions*, as well as the measured works of Aquinas, who patiently and contemplatively speaks, but more importantly remains silent when he experiences the "something more" that he had constantly tried to approach through his philosophical work: the transcendent and personal God beyond any mode of plurivocity. Kierkegaard's "fideistic shrillness"[14] is not so helpful here, perhaps because he is "also…secretly infected with the godlessness he excoriates around him in modernity."[15] Unlike Kierkegaard, Thomas provides philosophical resources to counteract Hegelian occlusion by offering a way across an otherwise clogged boundary between immanence and transcendence; which is to say that together Augustine and Thomas enable us to think of the porosity between religion and philosophy, which animates philosophy and at the same time opens her to the presuppositions of the theologian. The way across is that of the "superior," the "more" to which both Augustine and Thomas constantly refer. As I will argue below, each thinker achieves this by working with masks. Before doing so though, it is important to draw attention to and links between the way that both Augustine and Thomas think of divine transcendence as both "more" and "nothing." Such a both/and way of thought would perhaps be inimical to Kierkegaard, the philosopher of the either/or; but for each thinker it is important that the "more" and the "nothing" remain in tension, such that both can be spoken as readily of us as they can of God.

The "More" and the "Nothing" in Augustine and Thomas: How to Unmask a Dialectician

Two quotations, one from Augustine and another from Thomas, allow Desmond to think of them as philosophers of the "more" and so as companions on his own philosophical journey, constantly porous as it is to divine transcendence. Augustine's *nihilne plus* and Thomas's *videtur mihi ut palea* each speak to Desmond of the nothingness which is the "return to zero"[16] without which knowledge of God and of self, as sources of transcendence in intimate relationship to each other, are impossible. In his chapter "Speculation and Representation" in *Beyond Hegel and Dialectic*, Desmond

---

14. Desmond, *Philosophy, Others*, 159
15. Desmond, *Philosophy, Others*, 160
16. Desmond, *God and the Between*, 28–29.

effectively brings Augustine and Thomas Aquinas together, with these two quotations, so as to challenge Hegel. These particular "mores" and "nothings" are developed elsewhere too, particularly to highlight porosity, which is essential to philosophy and theology, as they engage together and with the world. I will speak now of Augustine and Thomas Aquinas in turn, as Desmond draws from them in that particular discussion, aware that many other connections can be made throughout Desmond's work. Considering these companioning passages together provides a starting point to find Augustine, Thomas, and Desmond in the middle space between the nothing and the more.

Desmond compares Augustine with Descartes, who "on the surface ... seems to acquiesce in Augustine's passion of knowing: *Deum et animam scire cupio. Nihilne plus? Nihil omnino* (God and the soul I wish to know. Nothing more? Nothing at all)," saying that the difference lies in this:

> Augustine will say "nothing more," not because he has clear and distinct transparency with respect to God, but because God is the "more" that ever resists encapsulation in clear and distinct ideas. Yet this "more" always calls for further unremitting thought, mindfulness before the mystery of the ultimate other.[17]

Descartes' mask betrays him; seeming to be like Augustine, by asking the same questions, he is instead other, closed to aspects of answers that will not directly serve his purpose. In other words, for Augustine the "more" is a mysterious openness of otherness, into which thought can proceed and from which it need not depart—so deep are its resources for the self in search for meaning. Descartes, in contrast, takes the self and God as a starting-point, from which to proceed further toward "the new science of mathematized nature."[18] Knowledge of God and the soul, he thinks, are easy by comparison. Descartes' God, then, is not Augustine's: it is no longer mysterious, and its ultimacy functions as a determinate boundary within a system—a limit rather than an overdetermined porous threshold.

Augustine's "nothing more" sets out a philosophical project intersecting with what we normally discern to be the domain of theology. He sounds out revelation to enlighten his innermost thought and being. This intimate interior self in relation to transcendence underlies all of his writings; there Augustine experiences ultimacy as the answer to his perplexity.[19] Such

---

17. Desmond, *Beyond Hegel*, 156.
18. Desmond, *Beyond Hegel*, 156.
19. See Desmond, *Perplexity and Ultimacy*, 11, on "the middle" in relation to Augustine's movement from exterior to interior, inferior to superior.

perplexity striving toward ultimacy is no less vivid in Thomas's thought, precisely because he acknowledges a "more" and also a "nothing more" at the heart of an experience of God's intimate otherness. For Desmond, Thomas's statement *videtur mihi ut palea* ("it seems to me as so much straw"),[20] and all that implies, becomes a reflection on the speculative thought with which he has been most involved. Desmond describes:

> Aquinas tried to reconcile Athens and Jerusalem, Aristotle and Augustine, philosophy and revealed religion. Moreover, Aquinas stood in the same tradition of speculative metaphysics as Hegel. Nor should his God-service, both philosophical and religious, be in doubt, even to a professing Christian. But what happened to Aquinas at the end of speculative philosophy? What happened was a certain enigmatic silence. There came a day when Aquinas told his secretary he could not go on; indeed his sister and relatives wondered if he was perhaps mad . . . Aquinas saw "something more" and said about all his previous thought: It seems to me as so much straw . . . Having seen "something more," he would write "nothing more."[21]

Unlike Hegel, Thomas's questioning and his great project of synthesis was always open to the something more. Contrary to Kierkegaard, Aquinas knows that there is value in stopping thought when it really can no longer speak. That is, Aquinas draws a limit that points toward something more, rather than constantly speaking of the "more" with words that might tend to lose their communicative power. Kierkegaard's great example of the silent man of faith is Abraham. If the mask of Johannes de Silentio reveals anything of the Danish philosopher, he feels defeated simply by looking at and trying to imagine the interior journey of Abraham, the father of faith, as he proceeds up the mountain to kill Isaac.[22] Kierkegaard wants to dismiss thought as insufficient before the forever unmediated and transcendent object of faith. Thomas, on the other hand, refuses to banish thought, but instead sees thought for what it is, such that "compared to the excess of its transcendence, my saying of it is as nothing."[23] Before infinity, finite thought falls silent—but there is something deeply affirmative in that silence, a "so

---

20. Desmond's translation in *Beyond Hegel*, 159.

21. Desmond, *Beyond Hegel*, 159.

22. See in particular Kierkegaard's "Speech in Praise of Abraham" in *Fear and Trembling*, 49–56.

23. Desmond, *Beyond Hegel*, 160.

be it" of thought.²⁴ The "so be it" for Desmond is the human ability to make oneself as nothing toward the "more." Desmond refers elsewhere to Mary's *fiat* in this regard.²⁵

St. Thomas looked like a madman to those around him, but he displayed idiot wisdom, in Desmond's sense of the term. This is wisdom that is so profound as to be best expressed in silence. His attitude and disposition represent a radical form of prayer, an opening of himself toward ultimacy.²⁶ Augustine and Aquinas bring together the "nothing" with the "more." Thereby they avoid fideism, and also the Hegelian both/and that Kierkegaard finds so objectionable in the Hegelian counterfeit double of God. They can make this synthesis because each has the personal experience that the "more" can be only known through personal assumption of the "nothing." That is to say, one's own nothingness is a necessary starting-point. The "nothing" is also a necessary assumption in this way: the "more" is so great that there is a point at which human thought is no longer sufficient; so that "nothing" describes what can be said at the point of transcendence. Religion is never overcome by thought; instead, what it knows, in its own way, is that which thought will never fully achieve.

And so, there is no simple contradiction embedded in the phrase "nothing more," which Desmond adopts with Augustine and Aquinas. Augustine wants "nothing more" than to know God and the soul, in the sense of thinking that there is nothing besides the "more" that is to be known. If I can but know the "more," he thinks, everything else will stand as it should be, as mere nothingness in contrast. Likewise, Thomas's "it is as nothing"²⁷ leads to the statement of his intent to write "nothing more." In place of writing, Thomas will be silent, but this silence becomes a mask, hiding and at the same time revealing what he has experienced and cannot speak—the "more" that gives thought its meaning, and at the same time annihilates it.

24. Desmond, *Beyond Hegel*, 160.

25. Desmond, *Intimate Strangeness*, 243n9.

26. Desmond, *God and the Between*, 133. Also: Thomas's mindfulness in this regard, as prayer, is captured not only in his philosophy but also in the prayer that he wrote, *Adoro te devote*, which in part reflects upon the way that the Godhead is veiled in the mystery of the Blessed Sacrament. A veil is a kind of mask, and so perhaps here, in this prayer thought as expressive mask, the theologian could also find a porous space for thought between self and ultimate other.

27. The radical nature of such prayer is in keeping with the nature of forgiveness, as each are enabled by the agapeic. See for this Desmond, "It Is Nothing." The essay draws particularly on Augustine's understanding of "nothing" as proceeding from agapeic richness.

This annihilation is, however, not akin to nihilism; it is rather embedded in an appreciation that creation comes out of nothing: it is only something at all because of the "more." In this way, the "nothing more" is a response to the "nothing" in relation to the "more"—an awestruck prayer of gratitude before that which makes the "nothing" more than it could ever alone have been. Let us see how both Augustine and Aquinas speak of the "nothing" and the "more" through masks, so as to think through the implications of masking for philosophy as well as theology.

Augustine's Masks: Clamorous Thought and Silent Love

Augustine's "nothing more" strikes immediately as a deeply personal philosophical project, working behind but also through the *persona* he offers the reader. As he masks and unmasks, Augustine's audacity makes him quite vulnerable. His quest, in its intimate dimensions, is unmasked when he gives us the *Confessions*, in which his prowess as a rhetorician (the practice of mastering masks) is evident. The *Confessions* works in several ways through masking: it provides a *persona* (the autobiographical character of Augustine himself); and it demonstrates how God presents himself to Augustine and us via masks, including that of creation itself. Thus, doubling is constantly at work. We, Augustine's readers, become aware of ourselves through Augustine and his masked representation of God; and this knowledge mirrors and replicates Augustine's communication of self through quest for knowledge of God.

While the *Confessions* as a text is punctuated with moments of self-reflection, and with questions about how and why Augustine is able to write his autobiography at all, one passage in particular is striking in this regard. It comes at the beginning of book 10, that great treatise on memory, and it captures Augustine's readiness to become as nothing before the agapeic otherness that gives himself to himself. At this point, Augustine has told the story of his conversion, and recalled the pain but also the peace of his mother's death. Having retold some of the most tumultuous moments of his life—brought them out in the open, through speech, he pauses and reflects on the act of confession itself. That activity takes place in Augustine's heart, because he is in the Lord's presence, but also "with [his] pen before many witnesses." Augustine may be able to fool his merely human readers—or at least try to do so—but such is not possible before God. Not to be truthful about himself, says Augustine, would be "hiding" from himself, but not "myself from you [God]." Completely exposed before the Lord, Augustine acknowledges that it is for his own benefit that true confession must take place, and the mode of proper confession is especially telling: "My confession to you," he says:

> is made not with words of tongue and voice, but with the words of my soul and the clamor of my thought, to which your ear is attuned; for when I am bad, confession to you is simply disgust with myself, but when I am good, confession to you consists in not attributing my goodness to myself, because though you, Lord, bless the person who is just, it is only because you have first made him just when he was sinful. This is why, O my God, my confession in your presence is silent, yet not altogether silent: there is no noise to it, but it shouts by love.[28]

Whether being bad or good, Augustine acknowledges he is nothing. When he turns away from God, he is focussed only on himself, with disgust; the joy of goodness is delight in having received all that he is from God. In either case, Augustine is "nothing." But what of the more? The more is spoken in silence, but a silence that resounds through Augustine as *per-sonans*, rather than as *prosopon*. Through him God's love moves, and such love brings with it peace that is captured more in silence than in clamorous thought. In the soul's most intimate moments with God, Augustine's prayers are silent shouts: love enables the more to mask itself, but not to *be* nothing.

Well might we ask then: why does Augustine bother to write at all, since silence seems so much more profound? At least one response is that in doing so he is praying, and one form of praying is to use words. With words, Augustine also thinks, making sense of himself, of how his life is situated within all of creation and the narrative of redemption. His life is also offered up to God, in ways that he hopes are completely truthful; for if they are not, then his words are meaningless. Finally though, he writes for us, his audience, down through the ages. For us does he take up his pen, and with it he fashions a mask. That is to say, Augustine when he writes of himself presents what he can of himself, in order to form an adequate picture for his own philosophical project. He wants to know the soul and God: nothing more;[29] and in aid of this he describes his soul in relationship with God. This seems to be, after all, the power of the mask when employed by

---

28. Augustine, *Confessions*, 10.2

29. For a discussion of this knowledge in *Soliloquies*, see chapter 5 of the present volume.

a philosopher who knows his limits. The mask stands for the person, who finds himself situated at the very limit of thought and experience, because in an intense and intimate relationship with what transcends. When Augustine's words have stopped, there is silence. But behind the words, there is a still more ontological silence: the silence of love, which can never exhaust itself—even in the words of prayer.

In one way, the intimacy of Augustine's life in and with God is unmasked in the *Confessions*. In another, his words remain an essential mask, as a mediating point through which we can understand anything whatsoever about God, and about the possibilities for any relationship with God from within the middle. So, in terms of Desmond's idea of doubleness, with reference to the mask, one could suggest this: the *Confessions* as mask allow Augustine to present himself to himself, as other; that is, he forms a picture of himself for himself, and that mask becomes another through which he becomes more porous to self knowledge.[30] That porosity, though, is only in operation inasmuch as his words carry real meaning, by remaining true to his actual relationship with God. Augustine, after all, is trained in rhetoric, which can be a powerful deceiving mask; of which the saint is well aware. To allow the mask to be true to its task, of enabling him to open himself to the "more" by offering a representation that is both of and yet more than he is, Augustine hopes to check himself. One of the ways that he does this is constantly to allow passages from Scripture to speak for him, through him. In this way, I would suggest, he practices the art of being porous—thereby remaining alert to aesthetic happening. Likewise, he offers a point of consideration for theology—indicating that there really are moments when human speech should be not be autonomously spoken, in the mode of *conatus essendi*, but be received, through the powers of *passio essendi*, as the gifted words of revelation.[31]

Augustine is constantly alert to what Desmond calls the "aesthetics of happening," whereby "givenness shines forth with its own intimate radiance, coming to manifest its own marvellous intricacy of order."[32] That is,

---

30. One can think here too of the moment before Augustine's conversion, when he sees himself as though a mask has been removed: "Lord, even while [Ponticianus] spoke you were wrenching me back toward myself, and pulling me round from that standpoint behind my back which I had taken to avoid looking at myself. You set me down before my face, forcing me to mark how despicable I was, how misshapen and begrimed, filthy and festering. I saw and shuddered." Augustine, *Confessions*, 8.7.16.

31. See in particular Desmond, *God and the Between*, 33–36.

32. Desmond, *God and the Between*, 134.

Augustine thinks of creation precisely as a mask which both conceals and reveals God. It does so by pointing to God in the fact of its givenness, or createdness. This, in any case, is one way to read another passage in Augustine, where he questions the whole created order, at first mistaking creatures for the Creator.[33] Listening attentively to the mask that is creation, Augustine finds that in being made by God, the world presents itself as a something that reveals its own nothingness; and at the same time its relationship to the "more." To Augustine's point that he wishes to know nothing more than soul and world, one might add this caveat: such knowledge is possible only because desire to know is set alight by the world in which Augustine finds himself; and without that world, neither the erotic nor the agapeic potencies of happening would touch him. Desmond and Augustine both agree on this point then: the concrete particularity of creation, in its elemental fullness, is a first and inexhaustible point for contemplating God.

Thomas Aquinas's Masks: System and the Sap of Mystery

Like Augustine, Thomas uses masks—but his at first seem less recognizable—less able to show the contours *through* the mask, of what is hidden. Where Augustine speaks of his experience of God, Thomas remains for the most part silent about the particulars of his own life. In the end though, each does fall into silence before death. Thomas refuses to write anything more, while Augustine wants only to be alone in prayer, contemplating David's psalms. Both pens take rest, but finally Thomas's more dramatically than Augustine's. Desmond has several suggestions about the masks that Thomas uses—for instance, the systematic way in which he presents the *Summa*, as well as his presentation of the five ways of knowing that God exists. One can also think of Thomas's insistence that our names for God are never entirely adequate; one can also consider Thomas's silence. Desmond sees the philosopher-saint's proclamation that "all is straw" and he can write "nothing more" as a mask, as a way of presenting the "more" that he has seen. In each instance of mask, Thomas cannot help but announce something more, because his thought is always open to the transcendent Other, so intimately the center and focus of his work.

---

33. Augustine, *Confessions*, 10.9. Augustine questions various beautiful aspects of creation, which reply that they are not God, but instead are, like Augustine, made by God. Their reply, he says, is "their beauty." Thus, a statement of the aesthetic.

Desmond speaks of Thomas's system, particularly evident in the *Summa Theologiae* as a mask in at least two places. The first has already been mentioned, in *Beyond Hegel and Dialectic*. In *The Intimate Strangeness of Being*, Desmond speaks again of the *Summa* as system, but now as a work misunderstood as solely system. "The *Summa*," he reflects, "is architectonic and systematic but differently so than the idealistic version of system." He goes on to explain that, unlike the systematizations of God by Hegel, Spinoza and even Kant, in Thomas's *Summa*:

> There is a finesse for divine mystery percolating through ... rising up from a religious ethos where, at best, the practices of prayer keep unclogged the soul's porosity to the divine. The sap of the mystery of God flows in the body of the work, though this is not always immediately evident on the surface, where sometimes a kind of forensic univocity marks Aquinas's way of proceeding. More rationalistic philosophers tend not to be attuned to that sap and turn Aquinas's thought into a Scholasticism closer to the prototype of modern rationalism.[34]

The surface then, with what appears like univocity, acts as a mask for what is there, running throughout the whole work. And what is there is a "porosity of religion and philosophy" mirroring the porosity of the person('s soul) to what is divine. In other words, the work as mask acts as an analogue to the person, especially Thomas Aquinas but perhaps also the *Summa*'s "witnesses," inasmuch as it allows religion and philosophy to mingle. Indeed, the work for which Aquinas remains most famous seems paradigmatic masked porosity. The human becomes a mask that breathes and speaks—allowing to pass through as its bearer speaks systematically of rationally held beliefs, thus using the tools of philosophy; while at the same time thinking philosophically always in light of what he knows most fundamentally to be true—at a very personal and intimate level. Thomas the believer is Thomas the rigorous thinker, and the clamour of thought never blocks the flow of God's life through and in his thought.

On the note of Aquinas's work *as* mask, Denys Turner has observed that Thomas as a person tends to slip away from us in his works. We know something of his character anecdotally, but only on "perhaps two occasions" did Thomas the man,

> even in his writings ... break ... through the impassive objectivity of his prose in an outburst of indignant rage ... Only very rarely

---

34. Desmond, *Intimate Strangeness*, 243.

would Thomas the teacher come out into the open personally, and then when the defense of his students, or the integrity of the teaching role itself, demanded it. On such occasions he was fully prepared to come out fighting, gloves off.[35]

Rare may be the breakthroughs, but Turner, like Desmond, detects something of Thomas's characteristic holding back within his text. Turner suggests that Thomas's transparency necessitates that he step back, so that his students are focused not on him but on what he has to say.[36] In Augustine, personality is on show, and that personality operates as a mask allowing him to speak. For Thomas, the text, wherein we see the structure and lucidity of his thought, becomes the shining mask through which we occasionally see him, but more so the source of both his speech and his silences.

Such silences are essential—and here Desmond, Turner, and also Josef Pieper agree. For Pieper, Thomas's silence refers not only to what he could not say when he did not finish the *Summa*. It also pertains to Thomas's "unspoken assumptions," the most primary of which, according to Pieper, is Thomas's "idea of creation, or more precisely, the notion that nothing exists which is not *creatura*, except the Creator himself; and in addition, that this createdness determines entirely and all-pervasively the inner structure of the creature."[37] Again, an inner world is opened up with reference to silence, so that silence becomes an indicator of both a "nothing" and a "more." The silence is no mere happenstance; nor does it result from descent into madness; it is instead a mystic glimpse into the "more." That "more," according to his philosophy, is not even what one would see in the Beatific Vision, but instead the perspective of what humans would have seen, had they never suffered the fall into original sin.[38] Seeing more is therefore seeing as a human was always supposed to see. Thomas's lucid text can be thought in another way: as a mask that aims to show the limitations of thought in coming to know what has been lost to us, through our first parents transgressing a primal boundary whose full significance they could not realize. What the first parents saw, one might say, was their creatureliness. They were exposed, and loved in that exposure: knowing "more" through the "nothing" because the "more" loved them in that nothingness. Masks in the garden must have been other to our present imaginings. When Thomas

---

35. Turner, *Thomas Aquinas*, 35–36.
36. Turner, *Thomas Aquinas*, 36.
37. Pieper, *Silence*, 47.
38. Aquinas, *Truth*, 1.18.

knew this, through experience transcending fallen sensory data, it seems that he found even his own magnificent mask, as text, insufficient. How excessive must this "more" be to strike one such as Thomas dumb, even after that same dumb ox had so prolifically found his voice.

Desmond thinks of Thomas in relation to masks: through the reasoning involved in two of the five ways. Namely, in the third way (argument from possibility and necessity) and the fifth way (argument from design), Thomas proves to be a thinker of finesse, rather than geometry.[39] There is, in other words, a subtlety to his thinking through these arguments that defies the limitations of mere speculation. Again, using the idea of mask helps to see this point.

In *God and the Between*, Desmond speaks about the third way as coming out of a primary affirmation of being, which relates to the "primordial affirmation of the simple elemental 'it is good to be.'"[40] The third way, says Thomas in the third article of the first part of the *Summa*, "is taken from possibility and necessity"; and he reasons that while things in nature can either be or not be, "it is impossible for these always to exist, for that which is possible not to be at some time is not."[41] For anything to be at all then, "we cannot but postulate the existence of some being having of itself its own necessity, and not receiving it from another, but rather causing in others their necessity. This all men speak of as God."[42] Desmond finds that, contrasted with Kant's "thin" appreciation of causality, whereby an effect is completely determined by its cause, Aquinas demonstrates that "if all being is possible being, ultimately all possible being is impossible."[43] From this Desmond derives that the other that Thomas thinks in its necessity is hyperbolic—and so, one might say, not the Cartesian God who merely flips a switch, but instead the God who "could never be a determination or determinate being."[44] For Desmond, Thomas's third way "has to do with being struck . . . by the incontrovertibility of being. There is a bite of otherness in thus being struck. There is no way to sidestep being, and the inescapability of its givenness, even if there is something overdeterminate about

---

39. For an explanation of these terms, which are frequent in Desmond's writings, see Desmond, *Is there a Sabbath?*, 191–93.
40. Desmond, *God and the Between*, 131.
41. Thomas, *Summa*, I. q. 2, art. 3.
42. Thomas, *Summa*, I. q. 2, art. 3.
43. Desmond, *God and the Between*, 132.
44. Desmond, *God and the Between*, 133.

being as thus given."⁴⁵ Thomas is, says Desmond, presenting us with what is perhaps "a thought experiment that tries to stun us into astonishment about the 'that it is,' despite the nothing."⁴⁶ Here the nothing and the more are in interplay. Behind the mask of a few lines in an article toward the beginning of the *Summa*, the reader of Thomas passes beyond, if she has the finesse to be nourished like Thomas with the same sap of a personal relationship with being, and through that with the hyperbolic. Such passing, that is to say, happens through the nothing with which we identify. Thereby one can progress to the more, which is overdetermined, and thus beyond systematization.

In *The Intimate Strangeness of Being*, Desmond thinks of the fifth way as working through the mediation of a figure, which seems to be very similar in his understanding to that of the mask.⁴⁷ A figure is a representation of what one is trying to see, or "figure out," which does not pretend to give the full-blooded richness of what is the matter for thought in a particular instance. "Our need of figures in dealing with God," Desmond observes, "often reflects our figuration and reconfiguration of the ethos of being. The premodern configuring of that ethos was more porous to communications between faith and reason, theology and philosophy."⁴⁸ Thus Plato can give us the myth of the *Timaeus* as a "likely story," which is far richer than either the "Hegelian sublation of figures into concepts"⁴⁹ or Kant's "as if" whereby God serves as a regulative Idea of Reason, which cannot be thought or known on the hyperbolic terms that relate to what it is (thought here against a plurivocal index) metaphysically, rather than only in determined human thought.⁵⁰ Thomas can offer the argument from design, whereby we look at the world and come to know something of its cause, because thought can provide a porous way through which the "more" that is the principle and cause of the "nothing" can announce itself.

Thomas argues in the fifth way that:

> We see that things which lack intelligence, such as natural bodies, act for an end . . . so as to obtain the best result. Hence it is plain

---

45. Desmond, *God and the Between*, 133.

46. Desmond, *God and the Between*, 133.

47. Desmond speaks of this way of "figuring" in Desmond, "Analogy and the Fate of Reason."

48. Desmond, *Intimate Strangeness*, 244.

49. Desmond, *Intimate Strangeness*, 245.

50. Desmond, *Intimate Strangeness*, 47.

that not fortuitously, but designedly, do they achieve their end. Now whatever lacks intelligence cannot move towards and end, unless it be directed by some being endowed with knowledge and intelligence . . . Therefore some intelligent being exists by whom all natural things are directed to their end; and this being we call God.[51]

All depends, here, on how we allow ourselves to experience the world. Thomas obviously observes that things work toward their good and proper ends only seemingly of their own accord. What he does and does not say is that what he at the same time apprehends is that God himself is at work behind that constant operation. Unlike Paley, the world does not seem to him mechanistic, and so God is not presumed a mechanic. And God is not simply *in* the world, contained in such manifestations, but is instead beyond it, so that Thomas through his very way of seeing and knowing the mask of creation, excludes pantheism. [52]

Thomas in all of his five ways is masked and unmasked as a human being immersed in the *metaxu*. In Desmond's words, his knowledge that there is something more, and of a certain ilk, reveals him to himself as a person who is "an analogical sign whose freedom and striving to be good" are "hyperbolic signs" that, taken with the potencies of self-transcending, indicate "ultimate transcendence."[53] The person for Thomas and for Desmond, thought thus, is a figure, as a way to figure out, divine transcendence; at the same time the person is more than that. For, if the person in her freedom exists at all, inasmuch as hyperbole is involved in the way she is given to be, then by analogy one can find out something of the source of such self-transcending. At the very least, that origin of transcendence must have an intimate relationship to transcendence as such. The figure here, I would suggest, can be understood also as mask. The argument from design, according to Desmond's discussion, only works when the self is able, through the world, to come to know oneself as self-transcending.

Let us for a moment place this person within Desmond's metaxological framework, and ask him to read Aquinas's ways from the *Summa*, penned for the author, before God, as well as for others including the reader. The potencies of masking thereby take on new meaning. For, adopting a persona and donning the mask by taking up the text and the argument,

---

51. Thomas, *Summa*, I, q. 2, art. 3
52. Desmond, *Intimate Strangeness*, 249.
53. Desmond, *Intimate Strangeness*, 249.

the reader can inhabit the world differently, with perspectives opened anew. Such invigorated experience, provided through the person in the experience of agapeic astonishment, is something that I will return to in a moment, because in order to appreciate it more fully, one would need to regard what it is to see as Thomas does—discovering through creation links to God, through analogy. Crucially, Thomas's *Summa* provides a way for the witness to his task to find, through the mask of text, possibilities for seeing that might otherwise only remain hidden. Thomas's "proofs," as well as his method for saying something about God—through likeness and unlikeness to creation—facilitate such vision, through a mask that mediates self to self through world porously known.

Analogy and Experiencing God

Such seeing leads to a different kind of mask, this time as expression of what is known and intimated. Desmond finds Thomas especially helpful, in that analogy mediates by doubling. Desmond's thoughts on analogy allow us to think Augustine and Thomas together. Methodologically in the *Confessions*, it is true that Augustine does seem to be quite different from Thomas. He speaks first of himself and the world and usually uses the words of prayer and Scripture to do so. Thomas, on the other hand, develops philosophical argument and language. Even with the seeming systematic sophistication of analogical predication, however, Thomas fundamentally agrees with Augustine's intuition that we are always between both the "nothing" and the "more." This, I would finally like to suggest, is the main way in which Desmond brings both thinkers together. To make this point, I will briefly describe some of the main aspects of analogy, as Desmond picks them up in particular in *The Intimate Strangeness of Being*.

As just briefly explored, Desmond finds in Thomas elemental awareness that is "severely masked" by Thomas's form of "rhetorical expression." However, excess again seeps through his thinking, rooted as the latter is in prayer. Desmond's chapter on analogy enables one to see how such thought, in the mode of analogy, is a porous mode of being in the middle. Analogy enables plurivocal speaking, and allows Aquinas to be true to the presence of God in the world. God is not entirely of the world, but inasmuch as he is the world's cause, something of him can be found in what we see and know. This is how analogy aids Thomas, Desmond, and us. For, being neither strictly univocal nor solely equivocal, analogy has the advantage of allowing one to speak of what is as what it is "like" and also what it is "unlike." Analogy, Desmond explains, "is itself a between, and communicates a between—and to cite the most important case, in the *likeness/unlikeness between* the creation and God."⁵⁴ For Desmond and Thomas alike, such speech is possible because of a fundamental relationship within being itself. We can only speak of God at all because he can be known by what he has made. When contemplating what it means to name God, Thomas Aquinas describes one of the fundamental implications of analogy:

> whatever is said of God and creatures, is said according to the relation of a creature to God as its principle and cause, wherein all perfections of things pre-exist excellently. Now this mode of community of idea is a mean [*medius* in Latin] between [*inter* in Latin] pure equivocation and simple univocation.⁵⁵

I have inserted the Latin in two places here to make a point. Analogy for Thomas is a way of intermediation, between beings, but also between thought and being, because of a primary ontological relationship between creature and God. We are, with Thomas, squarely in the metaxological, in the intermediating space where a certain attitude toward the world is pre-eminently needed. Desmond, Augustine and Thomas again agree, for, in the same article, Thomas quotes one of Augustine's favourite passages from Paul: "the invisible things of God are clearly seen being understood by the things that are made."⁵⁶ This quotation is obviously as much a point of reflection for Thomas as it is for Augustine, appearing again and earlier in the *Summa* when he argues that we can in fact demonstrate that God exists.⁵⁷ We can know and speak of God, the point seems clear, by looking at the world, by accepting what is given as coming from a cause that we can know and speak of—analogically. As discussed though, it is not enough simply to see; the way in which one sees is fundamental. That is, only by being "porous" can one find God through the world, and make and speak through the appropriate mask.

---

54 Desmond, *Intimate Strangeness*, 235.
55. Thomas, *Summa*, I, q. 13, art. 6.
56. Romans 1:20, in Thomas, *Summa*, I, q. 13, art. 6.
57. Thomas, *Summa*, I, q. 2, art. 2.

On Taking a Sabbatical: Being as Nothing to the More

Desmond's appreciation of doubleness and masking enables one to find the main ways he finds both Augustine and Thomas to be companions in thought. Each emphasises that only in first adopting an attitude of nothingness toward transcendence can any form of self-transcendence be accomplished. Such achievement is something received, facilitated but never entirely given by striving human thought taken alone. Augustine and Thomas both demonstrate what Desmond calls a "celebrating seeing," captured but never exhausted by their adoption of masks. This seeing echoes—and so proves to be more than sight alone—the "it is good" of the Creator gazing upon the mask of his own making.[58] And that moment of utterance of the "it is good" becomes the space which Augustine, Thomas and Desmond all share when they adopt the silence that deeply characterizes a "Sabbath for thought."

In his "Exceeding Virtue: Aquinas and the Beatitudes," Desmond emphasises the Beatitudes as "hyperbolic," "addressed to human beings in their elemental humanity," and requiring of us a "mindful porosity" in order to understand what the Beatitudes demand.[59] Moreover, the beatitudes exceed the philosopher's well-articulated claims that virtue is important. In particular, the first beatitude reminds us of our nothingness. "Blessed are the poor in spirit" refers to poverty not only as "a matter of removing impediments," but—and here Desmond's words about Thomas are very much in keeping with the earlier quotation from Augustine's *Confessions*—as "something more intimate to the naked soul in its exposure to God."[60] Thomas can take up his pen because he is alert to the need of such exposure, as a lived willingness to embrace the world as a means toward its maker.

This exposure opens up a manner of "celebrating seeing," which is in stark contrast to the "instrumental hypothesis that has to be mediated by evidences or sense data."[61] What will finally be seen, experienced through far more than the evidence of sensory information, is the peace of the seventh beatitude, whereby the peacemakers will be called the children of God. To know, deep down, that one is a child of God can only be mediated through

---

58. See Desmond, *Ethics*, chapter 5: "Ethos and Metaxological Ethics" (163–220).
59. Desmond, "Exceeding Virtue," 29.
60. Desmond, "Exceeding Virtue," 34.
61. Desmond, "Exceeding Virtue," 39.

the world when an attitude to that world, as also made, has already been adopted. The peace that follows from that realization is that of the Sabbath that Desmond speaks about in "Is There a Sabbath for Thought?," where peace is the rest that comes after working. It is a stepping back from the clamours of thought of which Augustine speaks. Aquinas's peace, alluded to in the Beatitudes, is according to Desmond a vision that "makes sense of war, be it social or political or economic."[62] The revelation is, for Thomas:

> not finally other than that of Augustine's vision of peace in the *City of God*. This is a multi-layered account, as deeply ontological as it is metaphysical and theological. Ontological: it is a vision of all things being what they are by virtue of an ultimate ontological peace; to be at all is to be in the gifted peace of creation as good. No finite being could continue to be at all, without some minimal peace of that being with itself and other beings. Metaphysical and theological: in that the ultimate ground of this ontological peace of finite being lies in God, the giver of all conditions of the possibility of being at all, and the giver of finite being in its integrity.[63]

Such peace serves here not only as a point on which Augustine and Thomas and Desmond just happen to agree. It is instead the foundation for being able to know and think and speak about God at all. An acceptance that peace is more fundamental than war, that goodness rather than its absence is our ontological foundation, provides for Thomas's *Summa*, including its five ways, as much as it does Augustine's move from the exterior to the interior, and the inferior to the superior. According to this Augustinian trajectory, the person is always the mediating point, dwelling in the center of a world, and open to the ontological peace, by being porous to what is other. The person's capacity to be double, by taking into oneself what would remain otherwise only exterior, is likewise fundamental to Thomas's rigorous thought.

Thomas finds in Augustine a constant companion in thought,[64] and Desmond finds similar nourishment from them both; and so it is unsurprising that such strong affiliations can be drawn between their ideas. For all the ways in which their masks are different, they rest upon the same

---

62. Desmond, "Exceeding Virtue," 47.

63. Desmond, "Exceeding Virtue," 47.

64. See Dauphinais, *Aquinas the Augustinian*, xxiv: "We might say . . . that Aquinas is an 'Augustinian' in the sense that, like all of Augustine's greatest interpreters, he engages with and elaborates upon Augustine's insights in a manner that challenges us to think afresh about the realities known and loved by Augustine."

foundation, which allows them to think as well as to speak as they do. All three know that it is only when one acknowledges oneself as "nothing" that one is equal to the task of finding what is "more." Thinking transcendence at its limits means transgressing the boundaries of one's own mask; at which point the silence of prayer remains. Desmond constantly draws from the springs of these saints because they are already thinkers of the middle, constantly porous to God's transcendent ways of speaking. Their elemental awareness is present because of that porosity, which is philosophy's true gift to theology. "The poverty of philosophy," says Desmond, "is openness to, porosity to the promise of an agapeic peace."[65] Beyond the agonistic striving of thought, there is peace; but only when the thinker, in the between of the elemental world, is porous to the agapeic promise of God's silent and masked love.

---

65. Desmond, *Is There a Sabbath?*, 349.

5

On Speaking the Amen

Augustinian Soliloquy and Shakespearean Porosity in the *Metaxu*

IN SHAKESPEARE'S SCOTTISH PLAY, mired as it is in evil that refuses to abate, there is a moment, after the Macbeths have murdered the king, when the main protagonist is on the stage alone. His act of soliloquy not only meets the standard of theatrical convention.[1] At the same time, he carries out the philosophical act of Augustinian soliloquy in reverse. This movement is the subject of the present chapter, and it sets the scene for thinking through the needs for individuals in communities, if they are to strive together toward the agapeic. Macbeth, in the moment that will be our focus, questions himself, and reveals how closed off he is to his moral community, how impermeable to divine communication. He cannot even pray, having found that when he tried, "Amen" stuck in his throat. This is but one of the forms of what Desmond calls "sticky evil" in the play. Desmond's analysis of equivocity in *Macbeth* draws from his development of a philosophy of the *metaxu*. When that concept of equivocity is seen for its indebtedness to Augustine's insistence on self-reflection, it brings to light that the true tragedy of Macbeth is that because Macbeth has harmed his kin, he can know neither himself nor God.

---

1. For more on the definition of soliloquy, see Stock, *Augustine's Inner Dialogue*, "Self, Soliloquy, and Spiritual Exercises," and "Philosophical Soliloquy"; Fox, "Augustine's Soliloquies"; Arnold, *Sololoquies of Shakespeare*; Hirsch, "Shakespeare and the History of Soliloquies"; Skiffington, *History of English Sololoquy*.

Read in light of Desmond's statement that *Macbeth* is a play "saturated with equivocity,"[2] the murderer's few lines of thwarted soliloquy illuminate the pathway of Augustinian journey both forwards and backwards. At the same time, such analysis accentuates the importance of self-reflection as an antidote to tragedy. Macbeth's downward spiral into further, stickier, evil (he is "in blood stepped in so far"[3] that he cannot stop) inverts the Augustinian order of knowledge of God and soul. Desmond's articulation of this shows how mired humans can be in evil when they refuse, in word and deed, divine communication. According to Augustine, when one journeys from the exterior to the interior, the self expands, so as to move further, from the inferior to the superior. For Augustine and Desmond, both moments of movement are needed: progressing from exterior to interior requires a sound and humble relationship to the world; extending toward God intensifies self-knowledge. At that point, possibilities for communication of transcendence, in a community with God and others, become possible. Macbeth forfeits all this with a murder; his refusal to stop there and to repent, retracing fully a journey toward his maker, is the source of tragedy in the play. Macbeth knows what he is at this moment, but he refuses to change. All this and more is better known when Macbeth is considered in light of the features of Augustinian soliloquy, and of Desmond's articulation of equivocity.

Augustine's *Soliloquies*

While the term *soliloquy* is associated with some of the most profound and self-reflective words spoken by Shakespeare's characters on stage, it has specifically philosophical, Augustinian roots. Augustine coins the word, because he needs something to describe a very particular way of speaking to oneself while in the presence of God. The freshness of this approach is highlighted by Augustine's astonishing moment of self-discovery at the beginning of the text of the *Soliloquies*. Labouring to find the answers for many philosophical questions directly related to Augustine's understanding of himself, he hears a voice. Where it comes from, he does not really know. Is it inside him, or outside? Is it him, or "someone else"?[4] That voice reveals itself as reason, which then makes certain demands on Augustine: he must

2. Desmond, *Being*, 112.
3. Shakespeare, *Macbeth*, 3.4.142.
4. Augustine, *Soliloquies*, 1.1.1.

write down his discoveries, so that an audience of a few can later read them. There can, however, be no such intrusion now. There must be no one to whom Augustine will dictate his thoughts; he alone must be the scribe. For the moment, there should be only one other listener. At this point, three are involved in the dialogue—all listening, porous to each other; but the audience only hears the words of two—Augustine and Reason. God's presence is constantly inferred, known by a degree removed, through the words of those speaking. Nonetheless, that divine proximity makes all the difference. Augustine truly knows himself only when he first opens himself up in prayer; philosophical investigation depends upon openness to God. As the text proceeds, Reason lays out the demands that are at the same time the agenda for the remaining work: first will come prayer that Augustine will have the stamina to find what he is looking for; then he must write down what he finds, "that [his] confidence may be increased by what [he has] done."[5] Finally, he will need to record conclusions. Augustine's answers will not only be for him; they will also speak to "a few . . . fellow citizens"[6] who, like him, are porous to divinely inspired reason.

These "fellow citizens," as we know from his later work, *City of God*, will be defined by their inner life of *caritas*, which is characterised by properly ordered desire.[7] Community thrives only when its members are able to love well. Augustine makes clear that a soliloquy can only achieve its integrative aims if it begins with prayer that orientates one's desires. Otherwise, the soliloquist goes mad, being out of synch with reality. This raises a major theme in the *Soliloquies*, which is that God heals the soliloquist's disordered appreciation of reality. The one who lacks such knowledge is unhealthy, or, in the Latin, "insane,"[8] where insanity refers to sickness of physical, psychological, and spiritual dimensions. Reason's role in the work of becoming healthy is to reveal, rather than conceal, any improper loves, or desires. Disordered love thereby equates with incapacity to explore and know the self with the powers of reason, which means that when Reason falters, or turns itself to the work of deception rather than illumination, it is an accomplice in foul play. It becomes destructive double-speak, turning to

   5. Augustine, *Soliloquies*, 1.1.1.
   6. Augustine, *Soliloquies*, 1.1.1.
   7. See, for instance, Augustine, *City of God*, 14.28.
   8. The Latin terms can be found in the original text published by James J. O'Donnell at http://faculty.georgetown.edu/jod/latinconf/latinconf.html. I am referring to these throughout to emphasize the way in which Augustine is playing on the double of mental and physical health.

the darker side of equivocity, which obfuscates, instead of finding and considering the potencies of selfhood.[9] Equivocity at its best discovers mystery, rather than skips over what one must honestly consider.

In other words, avoiding the pitfalls of equivocity means seeing things as they really are in their ineffability. To achieve this is the work of a lifetime, undertaken first with faith, and then hope and love.[10] Such vision entails true health of the whole person, directed by that person's mind.[11] As alluded to, Augustine's use of terms for "health" slips into equivocity within the Latin text, so that health, while referring to physical well-being, more often emphasises what happens when health of the mind is no longer present. In book 1 in particular, such health (*sane*) is a central theme. For instance, within his first longer prayer, Augustine invokes God as the one who neither drives his people mad, nor allows anyone else to do so.[12] Then, Augustine asks that God purge him of any madness (*insaniam*) and instead make him healthy (*sanis*). In order to become *sane*, Reason reminds Augustine that his focus must be on heavenly, more than earthly, delights. In other words, love can no longer be *cupiditas*,[13] driven by a soulless desire for that which will one day cease to be, shrouding the deceived lover in darkness, and leading to spiritual sickness. By contrast, the one with *caritas* is illuminated from within, by Reason that is virtuous—that is, well directed—toward its proper purpose. We see things as they are when we view their inner wisdom, which is their participation in God's love.[14] This heals us from an illness that Augustine thinks of as a kind of madness whereby reason cannot see what it must. Thus, the journey toward such sight begins with faith; one may not yet be able to fully see, but must believe that there is something there to see—a Beauty beyond all, which, when discerned, heals completely.[15] Hope is also essential, so that one will not despair at ever achieving such a state. Finally and most importantly, *caritas* infuses the entire person, turning him away from darkness and leading toward an

---

9. See Desmond, *Intimate Strangeness*, 51–56. There he speaks of the possibility of double-speak to be both revelatory and duplicitous.
10. Augustine, *Soliloquies*, 1.5; 1.6.12—1.7.14.
11. Augustine, *Soliloquies*, 1.13.
12. Augustine, *Soliloquies*, 1.3.
13. Augustine, *Soliloquies*, 1.19.
14. Augustine, *Soliloquies*, 1.13.22–23.
15. Augustine, *Soliloquies*, 1.7.14.

eternal cure; only *this* love never leaves, even when faith and hope are no longer necessary.

This is the quest for comprehensive understanding, where the eyes of the body are but a beginning point. Only with eyes that work, or are healthy, can we look—but Augustine emphasises that looking is different from seeing.[16] To see God is to understand him. This, finally, brings true health. Thus, the eyes look to the exterior so as to inform the inner man, who then sees what is above: God. This means that knowing and loving are the work of constant integration; health cannot be gained in what is excessively abstract. In particular, there can be no sanity when self-deception is at play. Augustine finds quite quickly how mistaken and hubristic it is to think that the mind alone can save. Under interrogation by Reason, Augustine proclaims that in particular the pleasures of sexual intercourse mean nothing to him: he is so much enraptured with the pursuit of wisdom that he has transcended these trappings of concupiscence. The next day, however, he is forced to admit otherwise, acknowledging what Reason is right to point out: that while he now experiences differently the imagined pleasurable activities of the flesh, they are not completely removed from his horizon of desires. This realization through experience, says Reason,[17] is God's way of treating his patient—by showing Augustine that there are still significant vestiges if what he needs to abandon in order to be truly virtuous, motivated by more holy love.

Augustine is devastated by what has been brought to light. In the darkness, he found something in himself that he would want purged. In the light, he can acknowledge this, but it is painful. He begs: "Why do you probe and pierce so deeply?"[18] This moment of porosity enables greater closeness to God. Brought to nothing,[19] he proclaims himself no longer capable of either taking for granted or of making promises. He thought he knew himself, but now he knows otherwise: that he utterly relies upon God to show him what he is. Until he truly sees the Beauty that is God, he cannot pretend to know himself. This is at the same time perhaps the most personal moment of the text: Augustine realizes that in this vision of

---

16. Augustine, *Soliloquies*, 1.6.12.
17. Augustine, *Soliloquies*, 1.6.12.
18. Augustine, *Soliloquies*, 1.14.26.
19. For the implications of being brought to nothing, or zero, see in particular Desmond, *God and the Between*, 28–30, 33–35; and the previous chapter in the present volume.

himself, he is the one at stake; he will be lost if he refuses to acknowledge what he would rather ignore, before Reason and in the presence of God.[20] This is a moment very much like that in the *Confessions*, where he sees himself for what he is.[21] As such, it reminds that the work of self-reflection is at the heart of much-needed continual conversion. This, then, is a moment of self-reflection and orientation. He had been so certain the day before that he had achieved a purity of spirit that enabled him to rise up completely above physical pleasure. Realizing otherwise, he is thrown back upon God, reminded of his need for the restoration of health. God's healing will make him sound in mind and body; it will make him sane, but only if he has the humility to work with God to achieve that healing.

Such sanity is brought about by divine illumination. Acknowledging his creaturely dependence on God, Augustine can know himself; he can emerge into the light. Thus Reason admonishes him to turn away from shadows, and toward his true self—which is imperishable, unlike his body.[22] Furthermore, to find the self is at the same time to find God; true self-knowledge only occurs in knowing at least something. In turn, seeing the self depends upon humility. Healing relies on us first acknowledging our darkness, our nothingness in the face of God. Again one finds the Augustinian order of movement: from the exterior to the interior; the inferior to the superior. As Augustine soliloquizes, he *looks* with his physical eyes, before *seeing*; realizing that he needs to focus on what is within. Such introspection helps him to realize what he is, in face of the infinite light and love of God. The more Augustine can honestly reflect, the more he knows himself as creature, as well as the debt of love that he has to God and to the world in which he lives.

Crucial to all this is Augustine's view that forgiveness and healing are only possible when one is honest with oneself. As is even more evident in *Macbeth*, without the healing balm of divine forgiveness, some morally significant, evil actions have the power to destroy every imaginable aspect of selfhood, including self-knowledge. This insight deepens awareness of the need at every point of movement, from exterior to interior, and inferior to superior, to be porous to the divine. As a general principle, this entails having the humility to place God first in the order of love. Practically speaking, it necessitates honest and rigorous self-reflection; and knowing when one

---

20. For a similar moment, see Augustine, *Confessions*, 8.12.28.
21. See also Augustine, *Confessions*, 8.7.16.
22. Augustine, *Soliloquies*, 2.19.33.

has breached a moral law and stands in need of forgiveness. One needs to think prayerfully and pray thoughtfully, as prayer and thought mutually disclose.[23] At the same time, such prayer and thought are affected by the exterior. A rich matrix of interrelationships is at play, such that a rupture at any one point affects the whole person in relationship to God, self and world. Ignoring this risks one's overall well-being—or one's sanity, taken in Augustine's broad scope of meaning. At the same time, it jeopardizes the health of the society in which one lives. For, as Shakespeare's *Macbeth* illustrates, an evil deed pollutes when it goes unacknowledged and unrepented. Macbeth realizes this sooner than his wife, when he is unable to pray—to speak "Amen." At this moment Macbeth seems to glimpse himself as he must look in the sight of God. He has the opportunity to undo what he has done, but instead chooses for an equivocity that closes off possibilities of communication. He is lost.

Equivocity and Being at a Loss

Macbeth's being at a loss can be explained in philosophical terms developed by William Desmond, who emphasises that equivocity refers to the manyness and the flux of reality, which derives from the overdeterminacy of being.[24] That is, being always exceeds what we can find, or determine, about it. We can therefore experience excess that occludes our ability to express and communicate. Positively understood, equivocity reminds that the world is so rich in meaning that no matter how much we discover, there will still be more to appreciate. Our use of language reminds us of this. "Words," Desmond points out, are "overdetermined; they mean more than they say explicitly, and carry around within themselves unacknowledged origins. Words are excess: they express reserves of meaning but also reserve recesses."[25] Put otherwise: precisely the strength of equivocity—the richness of its overdeterminacy—can be exploited, so that words can only seem to mean what they say, and the listener is left to guess the intention behind an act of speech. More troubling is that the speaker might hide from

---

23. See the previous chapter in this volume for a discussion of the relationship between thought and prayer for Augustine, Thomas Aquinas, and Desmond.

24. For the significance of overdeterminacy see in particular Desmond, *Ethics*, 63–177; Desmond, *God and the Between*, 35–40, 128–34; Desmond, *Being*, 63–75; Desmond, *Intimate Strangeness*, 38–43; Desmond, *Intimate Universal*, 400–404.

25. Desmond, *Intimate Strangeness*, 181.

himself through equivocation; further still, that a political climate can be so oppressive that the self is lost along with inability to speak freely. Here, equivocity can be as harmful, as tyrannical, as univocity, as the self becomes infected; words and reality cannot harmonise. Equivocity descends into oppressive double-speak. This is decidedly the world of *Macbeth.*

Again, such despotic equivocity has its counterpart in tyrannical univocity. It should be remembered that doubleness in speech is not, per se, harmful. Dialogue explicitly relies on such doubleness, whereby two speakers each present their perspectives. As is being argued, a prior doubleness is necessary to such healthy dialogue, in soliloquy, where the self questions and reflects upon the self. Thus the difficulty of recognizing oneself is emphasised precisely by indicating doubleness. In contrast, a dictatorial thinker can wilfully overlook ambiguity, and decide on one meaning alone where more than one is actually at play. This is where tyrannical univocity becomes realised. Desmond considers how dialectic can become dominated and consumed by a modern rational (Hegelian) univocal voice: the "dia" becomes univocalized to the point that the voice of doubleness is ruled out.[26] The difference inherent in doubling plays into an overarching synthesis that is then absorbed into oneness.

Dangerous in a different way is the refusal to acknowledge the doubles upon which the ethical dialectic rests. That is, Macbeth finds himself not *beyond* but instead *between* good and evil.[27] Shakespeare's presentation of Macbeth's world, Desmond argues, could actually form a response to Nietzsche's refusal of this ethical dialectic. Rejecting all systems, Nietzsche settles on the necessity of flux. In such a vision, all is equivocal—nothing is settled except what the striving will ordains. The relativism of the will to power refuses to find good and evil at play in the overdetermined *metaxu*. Nothing is determined already; and no action is determinable as either good or evil. Nietzsche offers us the unstable footing of Macbeth, who *wants* to be right that being sovereign in subjective power is all. Standing there with the murderer though, something else is apparent. Nietzsche detests the notion that the sovereign master should sometimes seek forgiveness and repent. Macbeth voices the despair of someone who *knows*, deep down, that he has "most need of blessing."[28] Listening to Lady Macbeth as well as to his fear at having breached the boundaries of ethical community, he dares not look

26. Desmond, *Intimate Strangeness*, 46.
27. Desmond, "Sticky Evil," 146.
28. Shakespeare, *Macbeth*, 2.2.32.

on what he has done. The contrast with Augustine at his lowest point in the *Soliloquies* is stark.[29] A Nietzschean might interpret this as the cowardice of someone unable to look into the abyss.[30] Is it not instead the case that Macbeth knows all too well that reality is not a state of flux overcome by acts of an amoral sovereign? This moment of ethical awareness is possibly the most honest in the whole play. Macbeth will not listen and without the help of an ethically aware companion—let alone of God—he is too afraid to look. He cannot see; nor can he repent. And yet, he knows himself bereft.

This brings to bear that dialogue, which relies on openness to the other and commitment to state as clearly as possible what one means, implodes when conversants withhold the real import of the words being used, or when they misunderstand or misinterpret what is being said. A two-sided conversation in quest for what is true becomes a disunity parading as robust discourse. Dialogue can in this way become monologue without the porous characteristics of soliloquy. The disjointed exchanges between Macbeth and his wife, in Act II, Scene ii, sound out what happens when dialogue is not porous to the self-reflective work operative in soliloquy. Out of tune with the ethical dialectic between good and evil, all forms of intercommunication break down. Destructive equivocity usurps meaningful dialogue. Augustine, Shakespeare, and Desmond all emerge here as thinkers porous to the ways good and evil announce themselves in the *metaxu*. Human action and reflection strive to respond to such communications.

Macbeth, Equivocity, and Soliloquy

Essentially, these three thinkers emphasise the power of language and the significance of words. In the overdetermined matrix of the *metaxu*, there is a real difficulty to strike a balance between univocity and equivocity. Overdetermination does not constitute disharmony and meaninglessness, but mystery and plenitude. Augustine theorises about the importance of words and communication and shows what happens when words open to all forms of transcendence work well. Shakespeare's Scottish play gives

---

29. Augustine, *Soliloquies*, 1.14.26.

30. As Desmond points out, Nietzsche has "contempt for the criminal who cannot live up to his deed." Desmond, "Sticky Evil," 146. The unrelenting Nietzsche demands self-knowledge that is at the same time knowledge of the deed. But he leaves no possibility for repentance. This is another way of thinking about closure to transcendence, and at the same time to Augustinian movement.

existential depth to the perils of miscommunication, of univocalized equivocity.[31] The playwright is acutely aware that when words lose their facility to resonate, all we are left with is an empty echo that defies meaningful interpretation. Macbeth is a fragmented self. Unable to discern meaning, he cannot become integrated. This, the result of the Augustinian journey in reverse, affects not only Macbeth and those who immediately surround him. His actions influences the kingdom and, he acknowledges, the whole created order, reminding that what we say and do always affects more than the self alone; such is the interconnected nature of reality. Reading *Macbeth* with an Augustinian framework in the background, and with the possibilities and potential perils of an equivocal milieu in view, throws into relief the implications of Macbeth's introspection. A close reading of this now will illustrate the implications of refusing to move from world to inner self, from lesser self to God.

It is illuminating to consider that equivocity in its more destructive form is at work throughout the various social dimensions of *Macbeth*, blocking possibilities for self-understanding. James Shapiro's analysis of the year in which the play was written underscores Shakespeare's personal awareness of how communities fracture when communication is impossible. 1606 in Jacobean London was a climate of fear; it was also the year during which a shift occurred in the meaning of the term "equivocation." From meaning simply "ambiguous," equivocation moved to signify "concealing the truth by saying one thing while deceptively thinking another."[32] Constantly in fear of capture, torture, and death, Jesuits attending to the spiritual needs of Roman Catholics still living in England argued that one could use words with the intention that they be understood one way by the human listener, and another by God. A secret treatise at the time listed four kinds of deception, the last of which argued that a lie was not essentially a lie "if you believed that God knew your thoughts, even if the person questioning you could not."[33] The very notion of lying is here contested, forcing a gap between what is (intention of the speaker, known only to him and God) and what is presented to others (what the hearer understands, based on the words used). This concerns far more than ambiguity, and creates fissures

---

31. See also Garber, *Shakespeare After All*, 700–771, on details of equivocation in *Macbeth*, and in particular on the use of "double" in the play.
32. Shapiro, *Year of Lear*, 178–79.
33. Shapiro, *Year of Lear*, 182.

where there should be continuities between intention and deed (here, the words spoken); and more fundamentally, between self, others, and God.[34]

The milieu of *Macbeth*, like that in London of 1606, could not be in greater contrast to that of *Soliloquies*. In the latter, Augustine deliberately opens up a space in which one can freely and openly articulate one's thoughts, beliefs, and even fears. There, in the presence of God, he strives for increased aptitude to say what he truly means. As a case in point, this is where Lady Macbeth systematically refuses to go. She chides her husband, telling him not to think beyond a calculus of who to kill, when, and how, in order to gain power. She severs her imagination, refusing to see blood for what it is. She declines to recognize the true nature of her acts, as homicide and regicide. These are the ruptures in the potencies of hospitality and community into whose gaping wound she descends. All this is done in the name of reason and of power—and of a love of her husband so disordered that it cannot be love at all. The lady speaks in tones of spousal affection, but raves with a lust for power, whose consequences she cannot grieve in the open. Her guilt, nonetheless, is revealed to others when she does not know it—in her manic, restless sleep.

As she pines and wails, the truth of what she has done emerges and engulfs. The Macbeths are both bogged in what Desmond calls "Sticky Evil." The crime may have seemed simple in thought—something that once done could be forgotten; referred to as a "deed" or "business" or "enterprise" but not as murder. The reality is otherwise: the murder is primal and messy, and it leads to more and more letting of blood. Right after the deed, Macbeth is the one who realizes this, knowing that his hands will never be clean again.[35] Lady Macbeth sees this only later. At the time of the murder she nonchalantly chides her husband: "A little water clears us of this deed./ How easy it is then."[36] Later, in the night, when conscience pricks, her underlying alarm can speak: "Who would have thought the old man to have had so much blood in him?"[37] We cannot see the blood on Lady Macbeth's hands, but it stays. Such stickiness, in sleep, brings with it nightmares

---

34. For some of the political implications of saying "Amen" in a religious context in the time that Shakespeare was writing, and with particular discussion of *Richard III*, see Targoff, "'Dirty' Amens."

35. Shakespeare, *Macbeth*, 2.2.61–62.

36. Shakespeare, *Macbeth*, 2.2.68–69.

37. Shakespeare, *Macbeth*, 5.1.39–40.

of hell[38]—a form of non-sleeping—for Macbeth, the clinginess of evil is obvious far sooner—but then even more systematically ignored. His is the stickiness of an "Amen," lodged in his throat and now unspeakable.[39] In both cases, a deed has closed off all passage of communication; but the porous passages of disclosure had already become partially clogged. In the face of equivocity, where fair and foul are indistinguishable, Macbeth has opted for what he wants, rather than what is. Sharp indeed is the difference between Macbeth's inability to speak "Amen" and Augustine's outbursts of prayer and praise. Macbeth cannot pray because he has refused to let the exterior speak with interior—by violating the moral order, murdering his king and guest, but above all another human person—and because he cannot acknowledge his own inferiority before the divine gifts of life, freedom, and goodness. In other words, now lacking his bearings, he can only be confused by what is otherwise the gift of equivocity.

The play thus demonstrates the problems of univocity when it is taken too far, thereby illuminating the balance that it is necessary to maintain between univocity and equivocity. Univocity is true to being when it reminds of the importance of forms of certainty, which can be spoken and lived. However, it is potentially dangerous, when it leads to one voice speaking, drowning out all others, demanding to be taken as the only determination possible on a given matter. This, one might say, is monologue without the characteristics of soliloquy. The Macbeths are in this way univocal tyrants—unwilling to listen to innocent, truthful, and warning voices, they silence through violence. The root of their univocity is in the reversed Augustinian trajectory already indicated. Macbeth's univocity is most evident in that he thinks himself superior; inattentive to the nuanced expressions of others, and in particular of the witches, he reads signs in the way that he wants to: his intention overrides any other possible motivations behind the words of others. Macbeth thinks he is able to outrun the supernatural; he prioritizes what seems over what is, to such an extent that no human life is anything more than "a tale/ Told by an idiot, full of sound and fury/ Signifying nothing."[40] The emptiness results from Macbeth's loss of self, which is first indicated very early in the play, after the moment of the murder. It is in these lines, when Macbeth, alone for just a moment, speaks, that he is most aware of what he has done, and of how he is now separated from God and

---

38. Shakespeare, *Macbeth*, 5.1.36.
39. Desmond, "Sticky Evil," 153. Also see Desmond, *Being*, 254n14.
40. Shakespeare, *Macbeth*, 5.5.25–27.

the whole of creation. He describes after the killing that he had overheard a servant laugh in his sleep, whereupon another called out "murder." Thus awake, the young men prayed together—one saying "God bless us" and the other "Amen."[41] It is as if, Macbeth says, they had seen his bloody hands and called for supernatural aid. Macbeth is terrified by this incident because he found himself, in the moment, unable to pray. He asks his wife: "But wherefore could I not pronounce 'Amen'?/ I had most need of blessing, and 'Amen'/Stuck in my throat."[42] Lady Macbeth demands that such stickiness, the result and counterpart of his earlier "screwing" his courage to the sticking place"[43] and murdering Duncan, must not be thought about. If they dwell too deeply on such thoughts, they will go mad. Tragically of course, Lady Macbeth does lose her sanity. Here, an unwillingness to recognize the full import of their deeds leads to madness. A healing double-speak is missing. She succumbs to the insanity that Augustine explicitly seeks to avoid. Where Augustine is willing to find and imbibe a bitter medicine, Lady Macbeth refuses to acknowledge her illness.

Also in contrast to Lady Macbeth, Macbeth can acknowledge immediately what he has done, and he realizes the effects of murder. The implications of his deed can be readily analyzed by examining his few moments of theatrical soliloquy in Act 2. For just a few lines, Macbeth is alone on stage, and what he says can be analyzed in light of Augustine's main points in the *Soliloquies* and Desmond's metaxological philosophy. Thereby, Macbeth comes into focus as having reversed the Augustinian movement of self-knowledge. At the moment in the play in question, Lady Macbeth has just left the stage to smear the sleeping grooms (possibly those who had prayed earlier[44]) with blood. Macbeth speaks as follows:

> "Whence is that knocking?/ How is't with me, when every noise appals me?/ What hands are here? Ha: they pluck out mine eyes./ Will all great Neptune's ocean wash this blood/ Clean from my

41. Shakespeare, *Macbeth*, 2.2.27.
42. Shakespeare, *Macbeth*, 2.2.32–34.
43. Shakespeare, *Macbeth*, 1.7.61.

44. Editors of the Arden Shakespeare edition of Macbeth note that while some assume those who cried out to be Malcolm and Donalbain, "it is more likely that they are the sleepy grooms referred to later [at 2.2.51], and subsequently made Macbeth's scapegoats" (Shakespeare, *Macbeth*, 180). If this is the case, and these are the sleepy grooms, then a breakdown of community is even more evident here. While they can pray, the inability of another to echo their prayer, or pray with them, is a foreshadowing of the violence that will be done to them by that same outsider.

hand? No, this my hand will rather/ The multitudinous seas incarnardine,/ Making the green, one red."⁴⁵

In these brief lines, several considered themes are evident. First, while Macbeth's soliloquy meets some of the formal criteria of that form of speech on stage, it neglects the Augustinian dimension, whereby one questions oneself in the presence of God. Macbeth cannot pray. God is missing, and so Macbeth cannot find himself. Secondly, Macbeth is afraid that he will go mad. Finally and decidedly, interior and exterior, inferior and superior, are all decoupled, because equivocity in its more sinister form has taken hold.

These few lines articulate that when members of a political community cannot pray and really be heard when they speak the truth, stabilising self-knowledge is impossible. Macbeth interrogates both interior and exterior world, trying to find and make links where he experiences only disconnections. The knocking at the door, the blood on his hands, the sight of the hands he wants to be clean, the image of a green sea turning red if he were to wash his hands there: all bombard his senses. What he wants to be the case simply is not. The contrast between how he feels—pale, literally "appalled" by every sound—and the red blood on his hands is striking, indicating disjunctions between what he wants (to be cleansed of sin) and what appears (evidence of his evil actions).

Then comes Macbeth's moment of true self-realization. In a gradual process of self-analysis, he knows that he is severed from God, and from creation. The greenness of the sea would not take away the taint of the murder. Putting his hands in "all great Neptune's ocean," no washing would occur. Instead, the blood on his hands would discolour every ocean. A few lines later, Lady Macbeth glibly declares "a little water clears us of this deed."⁴⁶ She demands her husband not be lost in thought. Right now, Macbeth can still think the deed for what it is. The moment passes, and becomes a rejection of guilty self-knowledge. This is the decisive moment when he closes off porosity between introspection and transcendence: "To know my deed, 'twere best not know myself."⁴⁷ To think about what he has done, in the exterior world, is to acknowledge what he is. He would rather not know himself now. Fully aware of the intrinsic connection between what he has done and what he is, Macbeth at this point decides not to be aware. He will do everything that he can to distance himself from the deed, and thereby

---

45. Shakespeare, *Macbeth*, 2.2.58–64.
46. Shakespeare, *Macbeth*, 2.2.68.
47. Shakespeare, *Macbeth*, 2.2.74.

from himself. The violence with which this invention occurs will, of course, only bring him further toward its inner source: his severance from God and Reason.

Conclusion

This moment of Shakespeare's soliloquy, read via Desmond's analysis of equivocity in relation to sticky evil, grants depth to the age-old philosophical maxim: know thyself. Such knowledge involves not only the self, but creation, and depends upon a relationship with God that witnesses to the fecundity of equivocity. It is the foundation of a metaxologically grounded community, and the source for all moral action. Again, Macbeth's inability to say "Amen" is crucial when considered from Augustine's main points in the *Soliloquies* and Desmond's metaxological philosophy, in turn influenced by Augustine's anthropology. For Augustine, the root of spiritual illness is the inability to acknowledge the order of being. Derived from this is the incapacity to pray and to listen to Reason. Further, the unhealthy one cannot define or communicate what is real and true. This inability to speak bleeds too upon those surrounding the unhealthy. One thinks of Lady Macbeth's doctor, who "thinks" but "dare[s] not speak"[48] about the evidence he has seen of sticky evil. Unequivocal honesty with the self, before God, is necessary for "sanity" and the health of an entire community at the same time. It is, then, crucial to this analysis to recognize that having reversed the Augustinian journey, Macbeth can neither pray nor listen to Reason in its fullest, most porous, sense. This enables a fuller understanding of reason's role in self-knowledge, and thereby facilitates a deeper appreciation of Reason in its more ancient, metaxological roots.

Namely, Reason in Augustine's *Soliloquies* is both univocal and equivocal—a richly metaxological interlocutor. Augustine does not know whether to think of Reason as himself or someone else, as interior or exterior. As a *dramatis persona*, Reason uncompromisingly drives Augustine to state as clearly as possible what he means and what he wants; at the same time Reason is compassionate and patient. Reason is porous to otherness, and particularly attentive to the desires of the whole person, as well as the communications of the divine. Reason helps Augustine to think clearly about who he is and what he wants. With Reason, his speech has focus and is directed toward God, whose presence illuminates what he most desires

---

48. Shakespeare, *Macbeth*, 5.2.5.

to know. He is porous to what he knows; it affects him as he receives it, and it changes him within. This is best articulated in his prayers—at the beginning his prayer is long-winded, looking for the point. Later, he can speak succinctly to God what he wants to know: only two things, God and the soul, "nothing more." Following Reason's direction, he prays: "God, who is always the same, may I know myself, may I know you. This is my prayer."[49] Thus, knowledge of God coincides with self-realization. This short prayer, the result of much labour, states clearly what Augustine intends. His speeches in the *Soliloquies* run in the opposite direction to Macbeth's language in Shakespeare's play, which becomes increasingly difficult to decipher.

Tragedy has thus developed out of a failure of self-knowledge that recognizes the ethical space *between* good and evil. This is a domain where transcendence constantly announces itself. Augustine's trajectory, taken in reverse, is applicable to dramatic tragedy only in a secondary sense. When Augustine, Shakespeare and Desmond indicate the interdependencies and communications between self, world, others, and God, they emphasise a deep mystery within the primal Judaeo-Christian story of the lure of evil and the destructive nature of sin. Macbeth and Lady Macbeth are like another Adam and Eve.[50] As such, they remind that self-reflection porous to transcendence and ethical knowledge is important for each and every human person. Only in learning from what I have been given, as it communicates to me, can I know myself; and only then can I see myself as I am—quintessentially desiring God. Two things only are necessary to know the potencies of being human: God and the soul. Such knowledge, though, is forged using the fire of an ethical life that depends upon open communication. Tragedy occurs when saying what one means, in the presence of God, cannot happen in either exterior or interior dimensions.

---

49. Augustine, *Soliloquies*, 2.1.1.

50. This is evident in several ways. There is a parallel between Lady Macbeth and Eve as temptress; the way that sin infects the whole world, about which Macbeth is very aware, as discussed, is another parallel idea. For more on this see Colston, "*Macbeth* and the Tragedy of Sin."

PART 3

*Citizenship in the Between:
Building the Porous City*

6

Love and Friendship in the *Metaxu*

Becoming Agapeic in Community

ONE OF THE MOST intriguing issues within Augustine's political thought concerns the relationship—or lack thereof—between the City of God and the City of Man. Thinking in terms of a strict delineation or dualism between the two does not do justice to the intermingling, on earth, that he emphasises must to some extent be achieved. Nor, arguably, does Markus's bold and influential claim that Augustine creates a third space on earth where both can operate together: the space of secularism.[1] Markus's thesis has tended to obscure discussions of what Desmond claims one can find in the *City of God*: "a finesse for differences of community."[2] The basis for such finesse can be found through exploring kinship. The implications of such kinship, for neighborly love as well as the formation of communities of erotic sovereignty as well as agapeic service, extend into considerations of what it means to be a true companion. The highest reaches of

---

1. For a discussion of these points, see Lee, "Babylon Becomes Jerusalem." Markus, *Saeculum* is clearly still the most influential text here. He argues for a sharp distinction, to the point of "disparity," between the two cities (159), quoting James Wetzel on this point (Wetzel, "Introduction"). Markus goes so far as to create a sharp distinction between the City of God in heaven and impossible on earth, and the City of Man only on earth. In a third space is the "secular," an influential concept in its own right, which it seems to me overstretches Augustine's distinction. Van Oort emphasizes the antithetical relationship between the two cities also. Oort, *Jerusalem and Babylon*. In short, both Markus and van Oort rule out transformation.

2. Desmond, "Neither Servility," 172.

companionship have a religious dimension, with Augustine claiming that the truest friendships are between Christians, who live in Christ and participate in the promise of the peace of the heavenly Jerusalem. These will be discussed further in the remaining chapter of this book. Meanwhile, this chapter will take us to where metaxological philosophy draws out what is contained in Augustine's thought: the foundation for hope in agapeic communities that already somehow partake of the heavenly Jerusalem.

While both Augustine and Desmond agree that a community is defined by how it loves, each is aware it is hard to identify—for all parties involved—where exactly one's most intimate allegiances lie. Desmond's presentation of interrelationships, instead of divisions, is readily identifiable, but scholars have often overlooked the same in Augustine's thought. James K. Lee makes this argument,[3] writing that concentrating on the eschatological significance, while ignoring the everyday ethical political importance, of Jerusalem and Babylon, can introduce strict separations where none would otherwise exist. The cities mingle, Lee argues, in such a way that Babylon can even "become" Jerusalem. Provocatively, Lee points out where the language of the *City of God* seems more to emphasise the differences between the cities; when Augustine preaches in *Enarrationes in Psalmos*, he stresses the pilgrim nature of the church on earth, and how baptism and the Eucharist sustain the earthly church's members.

The mingling of citizens in both cities is crucial to Augustine's vision of the way that Christians can live in the world, because members of our earthly communities are constantly *between* different forms of love. At the same time, they are bonded together by their relatedness to one another. A deep sense of kinship runs through both Augustine's and Desmond's thought when they speak of the possibilities, in particular, for communities where members become most fully themselves through giving. Augustine emphasises that humans are all members of the same family, and that the intimacy where two hearts are unified is the form of friendship that spiritually substantiates that point. This kind of friendship, *concordia*, is the basis for political life, and the root of the possibility for transformation of love within the political order. In turn, Desmond calls this agapeic service, which he links to the possibilities that are present in familial intimacy.

By exploring Augustine's sense of kinship alongside Desmond's categories of community, one finds that spaces for intimacy can thrive in the political order. Not only this: attendance to the possibilities of *agape* can

---

3. Lee, "Babylon Becomes Jerusalem."

foster well-ordered interrelatedness between citizens of the ultimate city. It may be difficult to elaborate—let alone inculcate—the foundations and implications for such a vision of political life. Nonetheless, each thinker proffers that our friendships with others, prepared in advance by familial intimacy and fulfilled in agapeic service, offer the best ways to live as political creatures. Essentially, Augustine and Desmond point out that properly human activity, in all of its dimensions, depends on that which is innermost, interior, or intimate. Hence, Augustine claims that the "inner man" cooperates with the "outer man," so that the spiritual constantly infuses the physical and at the same time provokes us to find the inner meaning in what we experience. Likewise, what we see, with our senses, in political activity, has an inner dimension, motivated by a form, or forms, of love. Similarly, Desmond contradicts those "politically minded people" who think of metaphysicians as "dreamers,"[4] and asserts that denying the possibility of depth in public life leads to a nightmarish state of affairs. Reality is profoundly rooted in love; the more self-giving that love is, the more it fulfils both self and communities. Such self-giving is *caritas* for Augustine; for Desmond, it is *agape*. For both, the urgency of desire, expressed in restlessness and *eros*, is as vital as it is continually present. It is there from the beginning in family life, where, amidst its messiness and frictions, we can learn to love, ideally in circumstances of trust. The relationships of child to parents, siblings, and extended kin, provide initial understanding of our relationship to God. Kinship, for Augustine and Desmond, is the basis for intimacy with others, and might ultimately be extended into fellowship with other members of the City of God. This chapter explores these ideas, and makes initial suggestions as to how intimacy in the political realm might be nurtured. Those recommendations are fleshed out in the following chapter.

Augustine and Friendship: Kinship and Cosmic Love

The foundation stone for Augustine's political philosophy is that every community is defined by what and how it loves. Likewise, Desmond calls communities "diverse social formations of loves,"[5] and considers each accordingly. This is one of the most crucial arguments throughout the *City of God*, which declares succinctly: "Two loves, then, have made two cities. Love of self, even to the point of contempt for God, made the earthly city,

---

4 Desmond, "Neither Servility," 156.
5. Desmond, *Ethics*, 385; Desmond, "Neither Servility," 165.

and love of God, even to the point of contempt for self, made the heavenly cities."[6] Major interpretations of Augustine's understanding of political communities tend to rely on what here seems to be a clear-cut division, between those who are out, and those who are within the most far-reaching form of community possible for the human person. However, these overlook another important aspect to Augustine's thought, which is that in earthly societies, these communities "intermingle." Thus the bishop states:

> Remember . . . that among those very enemies [of the pilgrim city of those who love God on earth] are hidden some who will become citizens, and do not think it fruitless to bear their enmity until they come to confess the faith. By the same token, so long as it is on pilgrimage in this world, the city of God has with it . . . some from the number of its enemies who will not be with it in the eternal destiny of the saints. Some of these are hidden, some out in the open.[7]

Things, then, are not always as they seem, and those who appear to be members of one city might be, or could become, members of the other. The cities overlap to such a great extent that they influence each other. Ideally, this impact would mainly work in one direction, with self-love converting toward its agapeic calling. In any case, that the cities can intercommunicate at all depends upon the interrelationships within being. As John von Heyking describes, for Augustine, "God, man, world, and society form an intimate community of being . . ."[8] This is the foundation for politics. Amongst humans, such community is perhaps most pronounced, because the human desire for peace is not necessarily reflected in everyday relationships.

According to Augustine, humans can choose for the order of love, but they can also fall radically short of that goal. To love with *caritas* is for Augustine the proper fulfilment of the physical bonds of kinship in humanity. Appropriately then, kinship between humans, both physical and spiritual, is central in Augustine's political thought—a point better appreciated when one considers that there would be no political order were it not for marriage and family. Spouses and their children are, after all, the foundation for intimate relationships, as well as for broader forms of political association. So it is that Augustine's work *The Excellence of Marriage* begins by stating

6. Augustine, *City of God*, 14.28.
7. Augustine, *City of God*, 1.35.
8. Heyking, *Politics as Longing*, 14.

that love and friendship—and, he will argue, the particular relationship of marriage, which is the basis for family—derives from the unity of all humanity as descendants from Adam. The first marriage, of Adam and Eve, is already a blood relationship—Eve comes from Adam's side. It is through that first marriage that we are all related to one another. In other words, the story of Genesis reveals that through the bond particular to marriage, we are all kin.[9]

The significance of the extension of this blood relationship throughout the coming generations, made possible through sexual intimacy, is evident not only in Augustine's work specifically on Marriage, but also in *The City of God*. There, Augustine argues that humans were created in a space carved out between angels and beasts.[10] From the beginning, Adam had the opportunity either to resolve to love God first and keep the commandments, which would mean communion with the angels in heaven and attaining eternal life; or to elect for self-love and lust, and bestial death. When one chooses to love God and others according to the commandments that are directed by the Creator's love, one recognizes that to be human is to be related to other human persons. That is, when we keep the commandments, we give to our kin what is due to them—and we become more akin to God with each other. This fulfills the social dimension of our humanity. Augustine reflects on all of this, declaring that God: "created one single individual" from whom he generated all others,

> not so that man would be left alone, bereft of human society. Rather, God's purpose was the unity of human society and the bond of human intimacy would be all the more strongly commended to human beings if they were linked to one another not only by likeness of nature, but also by the sense of kinship.[11]

That is, this blood relationship is given to help us realize how strong our social nature is, at an ontological level. Human community relies on the

---

9. See in particular Augustine, *Excellence of Marriage*, 1.1.

10. Augustine, *City of God*, 12.22.

11. Augustine, *City of God*, 12.22; see also 14.1. It is also interesting to note Konstan, "Problems," 104: "the choice between the semantic field of friendship and that of brotherhood or *agape* (*caritas*) among Christian writers was not a matter of doctrine. It depended rather on the felt association of the terminology of friendship with notions of virtue and equality that might be perceived by some Christians as alien to the values or sentiments they wished to express." Augustine, again, develops his inherited classical transition, transforming it through his understanding of what it means to be recreated *in Christ*.

fundamental relationship whereby we are all children of God through Adam. However, we can ignore that basis in reality and fall prey to the lures of disordered love.

Significantly, these innermost ties at the biological level find their counterpart spiritually. Together, we are a family characterised by being children of God. Through him, we can know each other—and the more one knows of self through relationship to God, the more intimate our interpersonal relationships can become. The previous chapters have elaborated how Desmond often reminds his reader in Augustinian terms, that the intimate is where God relates to each one of us: my self-knowledge will never exceed God's love of me, because the Creator is more intimate to me than I am to myself. In a good community, members are humble toward the mystery of self, understood through approaching the interior dimensions both of self and of others. Attending to another person in these ways demands a sense of natural kinship, but also awareness that the lovability, as it were, of the other will always exceed my capacity to know and love them. Focussing on the other entails the discovery that if one cannot even know oneself as God does, one can never completely cherish another person. As infinite self, every other person places upon me infinite demands. That is to say: I can never love them as much as they can be loved; as God loves them. This is, however, no cause for scepticism and despair; instead, it indicates the incalculable worth of friendship; loving another human, one is within the domain of divine charity. Based on these ideas of intimacy, Augustine develops the concept of *concordia*, which is the model for every loving relationship, including that of the self with the self. *Concord*, which in English is a synonym for peace, means for him the bringing together of hearts—*con-cordia*. According to the saint, it is the harmony at the basis for good communities. Going to the core of who and what each person is, *concordia* at the same time binds humans together such that spiritual unity mirrors divinely bestowed biological kinship.

For Augustine, all of these are essentially possibilities for companionship, present because friends are united by true love of God. Such intimate associations attain the highest level of peace possible on earth, and are thereby open to full communion within the City of God. Augustine finds that friendship of the natural order is already good, but divine revelation expands its capacity, so that friends help each other to strive toward God. For Augustine, *concordia* and *caritas*—or *agape*—are intrinsically related. His development of Cicero's definition of friendship as "an accord [*consensio*] in all things, human and divine, conjoined with mutual goodwill [*benevolentia*] and affection [*caritate*]"[12] expresses this point. Augustine changes some of the key terms used: in place of affection he recognizes *caritas*; and instead of accord, he gives us *concordia*.[13] Good will becomes stronger than the earlier philosopher could imagine: it is now the desire for salvation of one's friend. Friendship as *concordia*, rather than accord, is knowledge ordered by love, so that friends recognize the source of their oneness with each other. God unites them, at the innermost—intimate—level of understanding and feeling. Augustine realizes as a Christian that true friendship between persons is only possible if they both know the true source of love: Christ in his unity with the Father and Holy Spirit.

Were there space here, one could elaborate these points with a systematic analysis of all of Augustine's letters to his friends, or even only book 6 of the *Confessions*, where it is evident that friendships are crucial to his growth in virtue and final capacity to love God. One instance, a letter to Augustine's friend Martianus,[14] offers a glimpse of the dynamics involved in good friendships. Here it is evident that friendship can develop in levels of *concordia*, which increase in intensity according to how well the friends can love God. Martianus had been Augustine's friend before the latter's baptism. Their initial friendship had, fittingly enough, concerned human affairs; but Augustine now feels free to observe that theirs could never on those terms have been full friendship. Prior to his baptism, Augustine could not even be a friend to himself—let alone to another person. Now that he and Martianus are both Christian, they agree on things that are divine. Since it is always greater to agree on divine than only human things, Augustine reasons that their friendship coincides with but also exceeds Cicero's definition.

According to Augustine, because he did not know Christ, Cicero could not appreciate the reaches of Christian love. Nor could the Roman philosopher realize that when humans profess their common faith in Christ, there can be no significant human disputes in human affairs. Given that, in point of fact, Christians have and do disagree and fight, Augustine must have some very high standard of accord in mind. As Donald Burt observes, this cannot be a "bland consensus."[15] Christian friendship aims

---

12. Cicero, *On Friendship*, 6.20.
13. See discussion in Burt, *Friendship and Society*, 59–67.
14. Augustine, *Letters 211–270*, 258.
15. Burt, *Friendship and Society*, 59.

high indeed, reaching into dimensions of transcendence. True friendship, on these grounds, moves beyond Cicero. Such friends do not simply concur with each other; at every point of agreement, love is the foundation—where love of the other coincides with proper self-love and love of God. (Augustine sees all of this put to the test in his correspondence with Saint Jerome, which is discussed in the next chapter.) Finally, Augustinian friendship intensifies Ciceronian benevolence: I wish eternal salvation for my beloved friend; nothing else will do.[16] In other words, I love along with the love of God, according to the truth of the reality that is the other person in relationship to me. With him or her, I am a child of God. We are blood kin because we descend from Adam; our friendship is even more intimate when, through *caritas*, we are kin in spirit—this enables the entirety of creation to be intimately involved. For, as Desmond reminds, the *ens communis* is the foundation for intimacy that brings the whole created order into its scope.[17]

Lest this all be considered too exaggerated and ultimately unachievable, it is important to note that Augustine is far from idealistic in what he sees to be the case in human communities; his joy in Christian friendship is poignant because he knows the effects of love that has gone astray. Adam's fall has led to increasing disconnection between humans. Despite this fragmentation though, they are still "bound together by a kind of fellowship in one and the same nature, even though each group pursued its own advantage and followed its own desires."[18] When *concordia*, the bringing together of two hearts, occurs in true friendship, the promise of those primal natural bonds is fulfilled in spirit. This has significance for marriage, and for the communities that develop from marriage and family life. Ultimately, intimacy that finds its basis in properly ordered love has the potential to transform society, harmonising with the cosmos. Joseph Clair elaborates this point when he proposes that Augustine's understanding of community is influenced by the ancient idea of *oikeiosis* (in Latin: *concilatio*). This

> refers to the natural drive for self-preservation and recognition of what properly 'belongs' . . . within the sphere of one's self-regard, as well as a corresponding moral imperative to extend this natural affinity to ever widening circles of acquaintance.[19]

16. For further discussion of these points, see Burt, *Friendship and Society*, 59–64.
17. See Desmond, *Intimate Universal*, 396; and Desmond, *Being*, chapter 12.
18. Augustine, *City of God*, 18.2.
19. Clair, *Discerning the Good*, 39. See also Heyking, "Luminous Path of Friendship," 116: "[Augustine's] view of friendship as an expansive communion of souls experiencing the fullness of their friendship guides his reasoning about politics." There is, arguably, an

It follows that the better one's self-love, the greater one's love for others. This, though, is only possible through a relationship between self and God, recognizing that he is closer to me than I am to myself. Clair argues, in a work that examines household, public, private, and eternal goods in the thought of Augustine, that the saint thinks according to the idea of *oikeiosis* that the "good of friendship represents an expanding arrangement of concentric circles, starting from the point of one's soul and extending out to one's body (in health), household, commonwealth, world, and cosmos."[20] Crucial to *oikeiosis* is that one's self-awareness and self-love are in direct proportion to the demands of justice. The more intimate one's self-knowledge becomes, the more urgent the call to bring others into one's sphere of intimacy.

Of course, levels of intimacy, and expressions of those levels, vary in practice. It is one thing for Augustine to know that no one is actually a stranger, given that we are all descended from Adam; it is another thing to act on that realization; and quite another again for him to expect that every person will understand relationships in the same way. Recalcitrant pagans and heretics are unlikely reciprocators of fraternal love. Still, friendship is as necessary to a good life as health, and friendship is to be sought out and enjoyed.[21] In the truest friendships, my good and my friend's good cannot infringe upon each other. Furthermore, mirroring the intersecting concentric patterns of *oikeiosis*, the possibilities for such a deep love are configured in the early days of family life. The bonds of parent to child form the possibility for friendships, and ultimately for justice toward others. In Sermon 9 Augustine declares: "It's your parents you see when you first open your eyes, and it is their friendship that lays down the first strands of this life. If anyone fails to honor his parents, is there anyone he will spare?"[22] In this sermon, Augustine works with the metaphor of strings on a harp—each string represents one of the Ten Commandments. Laying down a strand, then, is like giving material with which to sing in harmony with the cosmos. Without those first strands, no music—no love—would be possible. Having received the gift of parents' friendship brings with it an ethical command, so that our capacity to love immediate kin provides the key in which

---

expansiveness both within and beyond friendship. What is *between* affects every form of relatedness whatsoever.

20. Clair, *Discerning the Good*, 39–40.

21. See Clair, *Discerning the Good*, 41, quoting Augustine's Sermon 299d: "The necessary goods in this world amount to these two things: health [*salus*] and a friend."

22. Augustine, *Sermons*, 9.7.

we act justly toward all others in society. Agreeing with the ancient thinkers of *oikeiosis*, Augustine knows that we are constantly in relationship. As a Christian, he both sustains and amplifies this notion, certain that Christ's love brings together all the strands of cosmic love.

Desmond regarding Kinship in the *Metaxu*: Familial Intimacy and Agapeic Service

Augustine thinks that every community expresses a dimension of the ontological community between beings, which exists because of our shared relationship to God. Desmond's metaxological philosophy articulates the same point, such that community depends on forms of love that are familial, distracted, erotic, and agapeic. Like Augustine, he argues that ways of loving are crucial to the work of selving, such that familial intimacy and agapeic service are linked and influence possibilities for the political order. Desmond makes the case that if politics is to be good for humans, it needs to work with what is most human—the self constantly formed in relationship to others. This entails constantly making space for the intimacy between humans to flourish in everyday life, both public and private. While our political communities can never achieve utopia, they can still strive for peace when the bonds between citizens are strong and rooted in the reality that humans are kin.

The basis for elaborating the four forms of community in Desmond's works can be found in his trilogy of *Being and the Between*, *Ethics and the Between*, and *God and the Between*. In the first of these, Desmond expresses that four forms of community can aid understanding what it means to be related to others.[23] When self takes the other properly into account, the discussion of selving—the process of developing oneself in relationship to "origin, creation, things, intelligibilities"[24]—finds its appropriate counterpart.[25] Without this, selving can take place only with reference to the self; becoming self-serving, it can fall into the trap of disordered self-love. Relatedness, Desmond points out there, is fundamental to the concept of Nature, a term whose etymology refers to birth—itself a social relation.[26] That is, being together is fundamental to being at all; and all that exists is

23. Desmond, *Being*, 417.
24. Desmond, *Being*, 377.
25. Desmond, *Being*, 417.
26. Desmond, *Being*, 419.

contoured in relationship to God. In *Ethics and the Between*,[27] discussions of community are crucial because one is mindful of ethos via ways of being together. From living in the ethos we come to know the fundamental goodness of being, and what it means to be good. In other words, goodness, or its lack, happens in communities that shape us. We are constantly involved in those communities, which offer concrete ways to know good and evil, trust and distrust, worth and worthlessness.[28] Desmond names four communities: the ethical community of family, the network of utility, erotic sovereignty, and agapeic service. Each carries with it possibilities for forming and malforming desires, and thus for making friendship either impossible or a lived reality; by being based on the self's trust or mistrust of others. *God and the Between* brings considerations of community to a higher and a deeper level, by developing throughout an appreciation of how God is the source of all communication and at the same time of the community, and communities, of being.[29]

Several years after the publication of *Ethics and the Between*, Desmond considers the political implications of these four communities in a piece entitled "Neither Servility nor Sovereignty: Between Metaphysics and Politics."[30] There he argues that: "All forms of community, be they called ethical or political, ultimately bear on what we love, as Augustine stresses, and how our loves are expressed and organized in ways of life."[31] Desmond draws explicitly on an Augustinian framework, in that communities are "social formations of love," where trust and distrust enter into associations that characterise the ethical community of family, network of utility, erotic sovereignty, and agapeic service. In another context, in the *Intimate Strangeness of Being*, Desmond indicates that developing these four models of community is his response to "a current Levinasian monopoly on ethics,"[32] which he fears can tend to focus so much on the other that it obstructs essential ethical aspects to which the self has access, such as "the

---

27. Desmond, *Ethics*, part 4: chapters 13–16.

28. See in particular Desmond, *Ethics*, chapter 1, "The Ethos: Being as Worthy/Being as Worthless."

29. Desmond, *God and the Between*, 150–58.

30. Desmond, "Neither Servility."

31. Desmond, "Neither Servility," 164.

32. Desmond, *Intimate Strangeness*, 115.

givenness of creation and the secret love of God."[33] Selving needs other as much as self, but not to the self's exclusion.

Furthermore, metaxological appreciation insists that ethics remain moored to its relationship of being given by and for transcendence. Human desire for goodness is ingrained as a love for our Creator, whether or not we admit this fully. Fundamental principles of Augustine's metaphysics underlie this claim that the source of our restlessness constantly indicates our origin and end. In the same vein, Desmond's assertion about Levinasian ethics— which is surrounded by similar reservations concerning Kant, Heidegger, and Nietzsche in the same chapter—underscores that the way a philosopher understands forms of relatedness bears upon how he or she practices mindfulness. Our ethos affects how we philosophize, so for philosophy to remain open to the richness of being, the ethos needs to convey the depths of what it means to be humans constantly related to self, others, creation and world. The first and the fourth communities—of family and of agapeic service—are the most constructive in articulating this. However, these can only be seen in their richness when set in relationship to communities of network of utility and erotic sovereignty. In each case, an analysis of the community on Augustinian terms brings to light more of what is at stake in the quest for intimacy as the basis for the political.

Nowhere more than within the family is it apparent that we are not alone; that we live in communities of interdependency. Making the same point as Augustine, Desmond calls familial intimacy the "paradigm for being related,"[34] because this relatedness is sustained by bonds of blood, which bring with them the various complexities of family life.[35] Desmond's analysis in *Ethics and the Between* emphasises the elemental qualities of the familial; our physicality is enmeshed in and porous to cosmic and transcendent influences. Through family relationships with parents and siblings, we are first formed; and then, we can begin a second family related to the first. Particularly in the first family, those who surround us constantly influence, without our realizing. The infant and the child learn about trust and distrust; beauty and longing; fear and anxiety; selfishness and giving way. Our appreciation of goodness is shaped and misshapen, according to

---

33. Desmond, *Intimate Strangeness*, 115.

34. Desmond, *Ethics*, 387.

35. See especially Desmond, *Ethics*, chapter 13: "The Familial Community of the Intimate: The Ethical Intermediation of the Idiot" (385–414). Also see Desmond, "Neither Servility," 165–66.

what happens in those early years when we have no standard outside the family, by which to judge whether the values we are learning are attuned to transcendent worth. Desmond refers to Augustine's discussion of infancy in the *Confessions*,[36] where the saint describes the jealousy and hatred of one baby toward another, for suckling at the same breast. Left alone with such monstrous tendencies, it is certainly not assured that each of us would find out what is good. As children we need education, training, so that our inner restlessness can seek out what it most desires. The alternative is to become mired in malevolence, not having learned to love. Still, it is apposite to ponder that in the same passage in the *Confessions*, Augustine reflects that as he drank milk as an infant, the source of that nourishment was both in his nurse's breast, but at the same time within the depths of creation, and ultimately provided by God. In other words, there is a rich and dynamic sense of relatedness here, at the very beginning of Augustine's life and account of that life. His experience of familial intimacy, even before he could fully think about it, was an encounter with God's agapeic giving.

In the background of their discussions of love, both Augustine and Desmond know that neither the convert nor the unconverted become good on their own; this can only happen to the extent that they learn, from others, how to love well. While the first family is the primary school for love, it is just that: only the beginning. In order to become an agapeic servant, one must realize that all humans are kin, in the full Augustinian sense. In this vein, Desmond's discussion of marriage as establishment of the second family, in continuity with the union of Adam and Eve, emphasises that only through intimacy can there be community. In marriage, two become one flesh, and others are born and received as gifts from beyond the united powers the parents. Another form of transcendence is evident here: the married selves exceed themselves through the offering of self as gift to the other, when the two become one flesh. Here, Desmond observes, *eros* can pass over into agapeic service, as one makes a gift of flesh to the other, as the other enjoys the self even while the self enjoys the other.[37] Forms of abuse can creep into all of this; and in Western thought, there can be a tendency toward suspicion of the enjoyment of erotic intimacy. Is *agape* tainted, or even nullified, when *eros* is involved? The enfleshed bringing about of new life, enabled through the equivocal urges of *eros*, emphasises that in their love-making the married couple are a unified form of selving, which

---

36. Augustine, *Confessions*, 1.6–7.
37. Desmond, *Ethics*, 390–91.

at the same time exceeds them. When children are received as gifts and not commodities, procreation's extension beyond the purely autonomous capacities of the parents is evident. We choose neither our parents nor our siblings; the realm of created nature stands in stark contrast to a culture of commodification. Commodification prioritizes self-satisfaction; in created nature, parents receive their children as a gift. This acceptance derives from love and happens in delight.

Throughout his discussion of familial intimacy, Desmond does not deny that distrust and harm, rather than love and nourishment, can take place within the first community. Still, he consistently links together familial intimacy and possibilities for deep forms of love in communities of agapeic service. For instance, he discusses that children force their parents to grow up, so that they can give offspring what they need. "This," he says, "is agapeic service in the flesh itself,"[38] as parents are rightly "worn down" in family life "by lack of sleep, by inconvenient squawking, by dirty diapers and pee in the bed. In the domestic mess, another kind of self is being born."[39] Much depends on that self, for it becomes for the child a measure of loves to come. Whether that measure is then adopted or defied, "we live as we are first loved," and without that first love, we may never be able to be "for the other in a genuinely agapeic way."[40] Parental authority, when it is based on love, becomes the model not for ownership of children, but instead for "agapeic service."[41] And, finally, when the family sets free a child from its midst, it offers a form of "agapeic release"[42]—the gift given to the other that is the possibility for self-becoming. At first, a child may not know the depths of such donation, but this does not denude its significance. The point when child knows what has been received comes at the moment of passing on, when child becomes parent; and then reciprocating, when caring for the aged parent. Each is an "opportunity of agapeic love,"[43] extending beyond utility, and showing up the impoverishment of an ethos that cannot give and receive.

In contrast to the realm of familial intimacy, the "network of serviceable disposability," which elsewhere Desmond speaks of as the "community

---

38. Desmond, *Ethics*, 391.
39. Desmond, *Ethics*, 391.
40. Desmond, *Ethics*, 396.
41. Desmond, *Ethics*, 403.
42. Desmond, *Ethics*, 412.
43. Desmond, *Ethics*, 393.

of distracted desire,"[44] does not accept the other as gift, but rather as opportunity for self-aggrandizement.[45] While this network represents the necessary move from the familial to the commons, the private to the public, it refuses to acknowledge that it is derived from the intimacy of the primary ethos, and so loses sight of the cause of human restlessness; the quest, but not the end, becomes all. Those caught up entirely in the web of this community mistake immanent relationships of trade for the most significant human activity. Desire is therewith "distracted" because members cannot focus on the true source of human restlessness. In *The Intimate Universal*, Desmond warns that the commons, while essential, can make us lose sight of what is intimate, as the world of work usurps true social meaning.[46] The commons puts us at risk of thinking that human relatedness is only about the opportunity for working, exchanging, and making. Politics also grounded in the intimate seeks to avoid that problem.

While the commons is a necessary space that, when discerned as derivative, need not harm, at its worst the community of serviceable disposability reduces everything and everyone to an exchange value. This usurps a rich sense of the private and of intimacy, and makes for an impoverished appreciation of the aesthetic, such that marketing glosses over true beauty. The network of serviceable disposability redefines Natural Law, which in the hands of modern philosophy concerns power, rather than the depths of nature; everything is reduced to its price, so that its transcendent worth is lost; and *eudaimonia* is replaced with the empty promises of consumerism. Finally, transcendence loses its meaning, so that we can no longer glimpse the horizon of the ultimate. It may well seem that this community forces all its members to abandon hope of knowing intimate relationships. However, its pretence that desire can only be about what is on the surface cannot escape the transcendent meaning of its source. Deep down, we know that there is more to us, to desire, and to value, than exchangeability. Transcendence needs to break through, if a richer sense of the commons is to be attained. To bring this back to Augustine: only then can there be true transformation within the political order.

---

44. Desmond, *Being*, 434.
45. See also Desmond, "Tyranny"; and McGuirk, "Eros, Power and Justice."
46. Desmond, *Intimate Universal*, 175–76.

Trust and Transformation: The Seeds of Intimacy in All Forms of Community

Augustine and Desmond both agree that the commons that constitutes the City of God can never be accomplished on earth. However, the more citizens know the fullness of the good, the better their public life will be. After all, our sense of restlessness can only be soothed by the peace that comes with knowing that we have "higher commons,"[47] which can know what "true use"[48] entails. Our telos transcends disposability and exceeds any terms of use-value. In *On Teaching Christianity*, Augustine distinguishes between enjoyment and use, claiming that everything but God is to be used; only God can be enjoyed.[49] The point sounds strange when taken out of context, as though Augustine is telling the self to use others as a means to final destination. However, Desmond's point here casts light on the saint's distinction: it is not that we are to use others and things for purposes of exchange. Instead, the use of every other in creation reveals something of the creator to the self. This is its use, qua gift to us and the extended community of beings. That created thing's value in itself is its usefulness for us. To deny the latter would be to forego the relatedness of God to us through our relationships in and to creation. At the same time, such refusal blocks any breakthrough of transcendence, so that art, religion, and philosophy seem unable to "rupture"[50] the surface of serviceable disposability, where everything has a price. That surface may appear smooth, straightforward and strictly transactional, but it cannot endure, because it does not deal honestly with truth.

Thankfully, transcendence constantly finds new ways to announce itself, enabling ruptures so that new possibilities emerge. Initially, these need not be fully intimate and agapeic. Erotic sovereignty can form a first bridge to agapeic service. Desmond describes how this third formation gives the opportunity for "excellence beyond utility"[51] that, unlike serviceable

---

47. Desmond, *Ethics*, 428.

48. Desmond, *Ethics*, 429.

49. Augustine, *Teaching Christianity*, 1.3–5. See the translator's note on this point: "... in telling us only to use the world and not to enjoy it, he [Augustine] is telling us not to make enjoyment of it our goal, our one aim in life. We have to use it in order to reach the perfect joys of our true home country. But he would agree that there is no harm in making the best of our use of the world, and enjoying it when we can" (126n4).

50. Desmond, *Ethics*, 429.

51. Desmond, "Neither Servility," 168.

disposability, does not deny that there is a telos to the human self. As sovereign, such community is over and above. It is also within the domain of the commons: a sovereign is defined by his or her public relationship with others. As erotic, it seeks satisfaction for the self; self-making is at work for the erotic sovereign—but this happens with and through the other, without reducing the other to the exchangeable use-value of serviceable disposability. A sovereign works for what is best for those over whom he or she rules; when this is not the case, tyranny instead holds sway. Indeed, this is erotic sovereignty's greatest danger—that the self could take over and absorb all forms of otherness. The sovereign mediates transcendence for the benefit both of self and others.[52] In this community, selving occurs because each self receives and recognizes autonomy. This mutual granting and appreciation is the foundation for companionship, which involves neither self-assertion nor domination.[53] Erotic sovereigns find in themselves that which is transcendent; thereby they can acknowledge transcendence in others. Still, there are risks that such a community can implode, as the self is crushed underneath the weight of self-importance that refuses to be mediated either by the importance of the other, or by the significance of divine, agapeic resources of transcendence. Trusting relationships cannot rest on erotic sovereignty alone—they need sustenance from what is more.

This "more," constantly intimated in all forms of community, is most explicitly present in those of agapeic service.[54] Here we come to the fullest sense of "commons"—where our divine origins come into their own. Agapeic service brings to a higher point of reflection that which is intimated in family life. At its more explicit, it can provide for deeper awareness and greater love: all being is related, and all being is good—because it has a transcendent, giving, loving source. This provokes, in those who are aware, a "fundamental gratitude" and an "ethics of generosity."[55] Again, Desmond calls on Augustine to describe in *God and the Between* that God, the light, is "intimate to us but is not us."[56] There is a doubleness in this: we are rich, yet impoverished; grateful, yet yearning. We receive our powers of autonomy

---

52. Desmond, *Being*, 439.

53. Desmond, *Being*, 440.

54. It can also be related to the "more" of Thomas Aquinas, discussed in chapter 4 of the present volume.

55. Desmond, *Ethics and the Between*, 489.

56. Desmond, *God and the Between*, 157.

from beyond. This, like marriage, is a "good kind of heteronomy."⁵⁷ Marriage and agapeic service are in the same communal realm.

As Augustine's letter to Martianus argues, and Desmond's articulation of agapeic community implies, the fullness of friendship can be achieved only when those involved participate in the realm of transcendence. Thereby, activities of selving happen with others who, like them, constantly strain toward divine transcendence, and appreciate the significance of knowing how to love generously. Those who have learned to trust within the realm of familial intimacy seem, according to both accounts, to be more readily predisposed toward the agapeic. This, though, does not mean that those disadvantaged in the beginning are incapable of achieving their final end. The metaxological approach clarifies this point, as being speaks to us of goodness; with, but also even without those around us prompting, we can become attuned to what creation has to say of the Creator. Any person can learn to sing in a divine key. This, for Augustine, is God's grace at work.

Augustine's image of the ten-stringed instrument comes from a metaphor used in the psalms, whereby the ten strings refer to the Ten Commandments. So, in living well, one is united with creation, to others, and to God. Such unification is the discovery of intimacy. Through divine bestowal it is achievable in each form of the community. Some, though, are able to achieve this better than others. As Desmond's analysis of communities brings to light, it is perpetually possible to find love in the world—and finally to attain the richness of the agapeic. This entirely aligns with Augustine's insistence that the two main communities are intermingled—so that one can transform into the other. Citizens of the City of Man are already learning the language of love, even when slightly off key. Their restless desire is a cause for hope. The final chapter will explore how such hope can be realized, but also how it can fall short of the fullness of agapeic love.

---

57. Desmond, *Ethics*, 395.

7

Intimate Friendship and the Christian Cosmopolis

Jerome's Challenge in the *Metaxu*

THE PREVIOUS CHAPTER ARGUED that Augustine's cities intermingle, and so provide opportunities for citizens in the City of Man to transform their love. That is, each person is potentially a pilgrim in the City of God; on earth, those who love well are in constant relationship, but also tension, with those whose love is disordered. This constant association provides a means for constant renewal. In metaxological terms, erotic sovereignty can become transformed into agapeic service. What happens, though, when those in agapeic communities—here specifically Christian communities will be considered—striving to be agapeic, disagree about how they are to relate to each other? Augustine is forced to face this possibility when he corresponds with Jerome.[1] As the two argue about how Christian scholars should engage in dialog, it becomes evident that they understand differently the rules for friendship between those who seek a common life in

---

1. This chapter deals only with the first set of letters that Augustine and Jerome exchanged between A.D. 394/5 and 405. In the series The Works of Saint Augustine: A Translation for the 21st Century, these are letters 28, 39, 40, 67, 68, 71, 72, 73, 75, 81, and 82. I refer to the letters as they are numbered in Augustine's corpus, rather than Jerome's. There are many analyses of the correspondence between Augustine and Jerome. Some of the most helpful in giving a general overview as well as analysis are Ebbeler, *Disciplining Christians*, especially chapter 3: "The Honeyed Sword: Rebuking Jerome" (101–50); Carriker, "Augustine's Frankness"; O'Connell, "When Saintly Fathers." See more references to further discussions below.

Christ. This chapter examines these letters through Desmond's distinction between cosmopolis and ghetto.

Desmond's thought provides a way to weigh up the implications of Augustine's view that while Christians owe *caritas* (a translation of *agape*) to all, it is important that they foster intimate friendships. His distinction between cosmopolis and ghetto, together with his argument that both are needed in political society, offers a background for understanding how Augustine and Jerome disagree on the rules for friendship. Stated succinctly, Jerome identifies himself with a ghetto, whereas Augustine wants to find ways to live as a cosmopolitan[2] with unique spaces of intimate friendship. Desmond's distinction aids in finding what these differing views imply for living in the *between*.

The space that Augustine and Desmond think is important for friendship to flourish is one of freedom. That is, friends require the liberty to speak frankly to one another; to take for granted that neither would wilfully misconstrue the motivations of the other. Such is their mutual confidence. Jerome has a slightly different view. Like Augustine, he is well aware of the classical notion that a friend is another self, and he makes reference to this in his letters. However, because he understands the self differently, Jerome disagrees with Augustine on what intimate friendship, of self to self, looks like. In particular, he can find no space for criticism between intimate friends. As has been discussed in chapter 5, Augustine's concept of soliloquy includes the need for frank self-criticism. Likewise, to criticize a friend is an act of love. In his letters to Augustine, Jerome presents a different self-understanding. He refers to himself as a warrior against Satan, and a veteran at that; his close friends, he tells Augustine, respect him as a figure of authority, and they defend him—particularly against others who pretend to flatter, only to then unsheathe a "honeyed sword." Intimate friends, according to Jerome, do not criticize. In the end, Augustine finds regretfully that he can only settle for a lesser form of friendship with Jerome: one where they agree not to disagree. This can only make any ongoing correspondence between the two quite shallow; for they are not able to undertake the labor of helping one another grow in greater virtue and in perfect love.

This fundamental disagreement between Augustine and Jerome can be illuminated by Augustine's major claim for Christian society: that

---

2. See Delanty, "Cosmopolitan Imagination," for differences between the classical philosophical meaning of cosmopolitan and the current political definitions. See Derpmann, "Solidarity and Cosmopolitanism," for a discussion of how these concepts might still be related to one another in contemporary political theory.

Christians need to nourish particular friendships, while fulfilling the universal command to love each person one meets as neighbour and as kin.³ He seems, therefore, somewhat taken aback when, upon entering into correspondence with Saint Jerome, he discovers that the norms for interactions between Christians are not always to be taken for granted. Augustine initially writes to Jerome that since they are brothers in Christ, with at least one dear friend in common, they can already depend upon having close friendship.⁴ Distance should not stand in their way, because through letters they can carry out some of the most essential activities of friendship: a symmetrical, reciprocal exchange of ideas—including mutual correction where necessary—so that they can both come further toward the truth. Jerome's responses force Augustine to reconsider his idealized notions of what Christians can expect from each other; to re-evaluate the difference distance makes, and to modify his own way of criticizing a brother in Christ. His exchanges with Jerome offer a rare view of a Christian seeking balance between the universal demands of a cosmopolis (where certain virtues are demanded of all) and a ghetto (where a restricted community agrees on certain virtues not, as a matter of course, accepted by others outside).

William Desmond's distinction, in *The Intimate Universal*, between cosmopolis and ghetto is particularly relevant here for the relation that it bears to his appreciation of what it means to have a companion in thought.⁵ For Desmond, such companions—the two instances of Augustine and Thomas Aquinas have been discussed in chapter 4 of this book—are scholars he has not met in person. Furthermore, he has not necessarily read the entirety of their work. Yet, with them he enjoys a bond of community. Desmond's idea of what is essentially scholarly and spiritual companionship enables one to see some of the trademarks for a community of companions that can be intimate while striving for what is universal between humans. Some of these characteristics overlap with the criteria for friendship that Augustine expects from Jerome. For instance, such a community can form across not only space (as was the case for Augustine and Jerome), but also time (between, for instance, Desmond, Augustine, and Thomas—and others⁶). Furthermore, in order truly to be open to all, a community of

---

3. For the cosmopolitan dimensions of this, see Gregory, *Politics*, 293–98. Also see Burt, *Friendship and Society*, 66–67.

4. Augustine, *Letters 1–99*, 28.1.1.

5. Desmond, *Intimate Universal*, 26–30.

6. One thinks for instance, in Desmond's work, of Plato, Aristotle, Pascal, and

Christian scholars needs to recognize all members (potential and actual) as equal; but if it is to foster intimacy, it cannot insist on superficial sameness. Augustine takes for granted that Jerome will agree on the meaning and practices of Christian fellowship, especially because of their common love of reading and interpreting Scripture. He learns that he cannot be so confident.

Discouragingly, the demands that Augustine places on the ideal scholarly and spiritual friendship are unacceptable to Jerome. Jerome insists that scholarship and philology are the primary modes for engaging with Scripture; Augustine has a more pastoral emphasis, while still insisting on and delighting in such study.[7] Crucially, Jerome cannot accept Augustine's frankness; and this indicates a different understanding of the modes of intimacy that Christians can have with each other, both in person and from afar. Augustine claims that distance should not abrogate the fullness of such a friendship, and that its participants form part of a larger community. In other words, Augustine seems to think that Aristotle's claim that *philoi* of the best kind need to live in proximity, should not be absolutely necessary for Christians, who hold a common worldview that rely on spiritual modes of development and interaction.[8] This means that letters and other shared texts can do the work that would otherwise be impossible for those in the far-flung places of the earth. With the exchange of ideas, scholarly Christian friends can help each other to achieve excellence in moral

---

Kierkegaard; and also in another way of Nietzsche. Descartes, Hegel, and Kant are examples of thinkers who provoke thought, but one does not discern the same sense of companionship with these.

7. The particular instance that Augustine brings to Jerome's attention in this regard is a translation of a word in the book of Jonah. Jerome has found that a word meaning "gourd" would be more appropriate than "ivy." When the new translation is read out to a congregation in Augustine's diocese, there is quite literally a riot. Augustine offers the opinion that it will be good, given such incidents, if Jerome's translation did not become the standard for everyone—it would distract from the message of Scripture. Jerome retorts that his translation is accurate; but this misses Augustine's pastoral point. See Augustine, *Letters 1–99*, 71.3.5; 75.21; 82.35. Also see Carriker, "Augustine's Frankness," 132: "Grützmacher does not notice that, 'although Augustine's chivalry and modesty kept his relationships with Jerome civil . . . his higher purpose was to determine answers to specific theological problems, because solving these problems brings men closer to God."

8. Nussbaum, *Fragility*, 358. See Ebbeler, *Disciplining Christians*, 7, for her thesis that Augustine seeks to broaden the horizons of Christian friendship by taking it into letter-writing; thus proximity is not a *sine qua non* of intimate friendship, though it is highly desirable.

Intimate Friendship and the Christian Cosmopolis

virtue—particularly when contemplating Scripture.[9] The challenge in all of this is to strive toward a universally acceptable mode of discourse that is still a conversation that has the marks of close friendship. Augustine and Desmond both converse with those who are local and contemporary; they address those of the past, and engage with those whom they have not met, with whom they seek, and sometimes find, genuine concord grounded in common desire for the truth.

Jerome is by no means so certain that all of this is possible; and his reticence seems to have two causes: the problems of distance, and the distrust of those who claim to be friends but who criticize his work. Augustine could not have known that his letters would arrive in Bethlehem at a moment when Jerome had vehemently and publicly brought one of his most intimate friendships to an end. One can almost hear the sharp intake of breath in Hippo, as what he has done dawns on Augustine—he has reopened the wound inflicted by an intimate friend turned into an enemy.[10] Jerome has, as a kind of warning, sent him the tract he wrote against Rufinus, and the raw experience of a friend become an enemy is evident.[11] Augustine finds the tract a chilling read.[12] As Desmond observes in *Is There a Sabbath for Thought?*, a friendship that is beyond redemption is a kind of death that can no longer call upon the life-giving energies that nourish *philoi* and agapeic servants.[13] Augustine grieves at the loss of intimacy between Jerome and Rufinus, and expresses a fear that he too will become the subject of Jerome's wrath. Such rage would seem to admit of no forgiveness, no re-establishment of the intimacy of concord.[14]

In what follows, this chapter will draw from Desmond's discussion of cosmopolis and ghetto, together with his ideas about companionship and enemies, to explore Augustine's attempted friendship with Jerome. Thereby, it fleshes out some of the possibilities for friendships that are both cosmopolitan and intimate. At the same time, it seeks guidelines for the written interactions between contemporary scholars, if they are to succeed

---

9. The paradigmatic case for Christians contemplating Scripture together and coming closer to God thereby is of course in person, rather than at a distance. For a full discussion on the role of this in Augustine's thought, see Vessey, "Conference and Confession."

10. See Jamieson, "Stesichoran Palinode," 362.

11. Jerome sends this with his letter 68; Augustine responds in letter 73.

12. Augustine, *Letters 1–99*, 73.8–9.

13. Desmond, "Enemies," 304–5.

14. Augustine, *Letters 1–99*, 73.10: ". . . it will be reason for joy and for much greater joy if you return from such hostilities to your original oneness of heart."

in striving toward agapeic communities. Like Augustine and Jerome, scholars today can often converse only via written communication. The speed with which words are written and then conveyed would be unimaginable in the fourth century; and this places further pressure on what and how we write to one another. Often too, what is written is quite public; and when Christians argue, this can sometimes be a cause for scandal. Both Augustine and Jerome were concerned with such issues. Augustine's insistence on frankness in friendship is difficult to navigate, when distance and possible interception and publication of private letters is a constant threat. Bearing all this in mind, this ancient dispute still has much to teach us now.

Interpreting Disputes between Peter and Paul, Jerome and Augustine

To theorize about friendships is one thing, and the basis for such investigation has been discussed to an extent in the previous chapter. Actually to be a friend is something more, and on occasion something else. An avenue to appreciate Augustine's approach to the importance of friendship is to examine how he pursues and keeps friendships throughout his life. In fact, such studies have been undertaken by others, and are in the background of this chapter.[15] Here, another approach is undertaken, which is to explore an extended moment where Augustine aims at but, according to his own standards, falls short of the fullness of friendship with a fellow Christian scholar. The main substance of their dispute is an incident in *Galatians* where Saint Paul publicly reprimands Saint Peter. Augustine interprets that Paul achieves his Christian goal of frankly reprimanding a fellow Christian, and that the Church is better for the altercation. Jerome instead thinks that Peter could not possibly have been wrong, and that Paul must not really have challenged someone superior in the hierarchy of the church. He adopts Origen's theory of a useful lie[16] in order to explain. There are here already some indications that that Jerome thinks of relationships in terms of hierarchy and obedience; whereas Augustine fosters a more egalitarian understanding for associations between Christians. Augustine's concerns

---

15. See for instance McNamara, *Friendship in Saint Augustine*; and McNamara, *Friends and Friendship for Augustine*. Also see Burt, *Friendship and Society*; Nawar, "Augustine on the Dangers"; Clair, *Discerning the Good*.

16. This is what Augustine calls it, especially throughout letter 82 (Augustine, *Letters 1–99*, 82).

when reading Scripture are, in the end, more pastorally oriented. Scholarship is important, but it is in service of a relationship with Christ.[17]

There are two sets of letters between Augustine and Jerome, and it is in the first that they establish that they disagree on the role of frank criticism in friendship. Since Paul's Letter to the Galatians 2:11–14 is a touchstone in the dispute between Augustine and Jerome, reviewing it in more detail provides some context. There, Saint Paul recounts that he reprimanded Saint Peter at Antioch—an exemplary moment of frank criticism, in Augustine's estimation. The first of the apostles, Paul describes, had begun to eat only according to the customs of the Jews and not the Gentiles; not only this, but he was demanding that other Christians (including non-Jews) do the same, causing a misunderstanding of the new law for Christians. This, Saint Paul claimed publicly to Peter, was a form of hypocrisy, and at the same time a refusal to recognize in action that the old Law has been abolished to make way for the new, inaugurated by Christ.

To employ here Desmond's categories for thinking through political implications in the *metaxu*, one might say the following. Paul argues here in cosmopolitan terms, having discerned that Peter is acting as though he is in a ghetto. As Desmond outlines:

> Cosmopolis, it seems, is open to the whole, tolerant of all, fostering, as an ideal, the universal citizen of the totality . . . The ghetto, by comparison, is inhabited by dwellers who are turned into a confined community that . . . is marked by a certain (perhaps forced) clinging to its own totality.[18]

On one side, the cosmopolis seems to accept all forms of otherness, while the ghetto is "hostile" to what might be other. Peter, in such an approximation, is far from cosmopolitan in *Galatians*. A certain recalcitrance comes to bear, as he retreats to what he knows, to where he is comfortable. The certainties that come with being in the ghetto cannot be denied. In their familiarity, they confirm identity in a living community. The intimacies of eating rituals, amongst those who have grown up and lived together in the same way as each other are, after all, difficult to cast away. This, as Paul

---

17. On this see Ebbeler, *Disciplining Christians*, 122–23. Also see Williams, "Politics and the Soul," 65: Augustine prefers to think of the Christian commonwealth not in terms of pagan governance and glory, but instead as "ideally, a pastor reality, its ruler a director of souls."

18. Desmond, *Intimate Universal*, 26.

realizes, is precisely one of the challenges for the "new man," which is to say the Christian striving to live in agapeic communities.

Paul challenges Peter's behaviour as an affront to the universality of the Christian message. Not only this; he remonstrates Peter in public rather than in private, so that all can learn from this moment of teaching. The demands to keep only to the Jewish laws surrounding eating really have been overthrown; in Christianity, something new is happening, and to deny this is to reject the difference that Christ makes in our lives. This newness is a major theme that Augustine extracts from all of Paul's letters. It relates to Paul's following argument in *Galatians*, that justification is now through faith first of all.[19] This is the reason, Paul emphasises, that the Old Law, while not harmful, is insufficient, and ultimately ineffective. From Paul's perspective, Peter can eat with the Jews or not eat with them. This in itself makes no difference. However, for Peter to pretend to his followers that Christians cannot eat with the gentiles and must keep to Jewish eating rituals is misleading and spiritually dangerous.

Paul does not tell the Galatians, in this letter at least, how Peter responded to his chastisement, and Augustine seems to assume that Peter accepts the truth in humility and mends his ways. Jerome, on the other hand, finds it outrageous that Paul would publicly reprimand Peter, who has seniority over all of the apostles. He therefore chooses—taking his lead from others before him—to interpret that the whole incident was staged by Peter and Paul.[20] According to Jerome, Peter and Paul used this moment to teach those who had been doing the wrong thing, without singling out any one of them. This, again, is the crux of Augustine's criticism of Jerome. Namely, he claims that Jerome is saying that Paul, and thus the inspired word of Scripture, has lied. As a hermeneutical maxim, Augustine declares, Scripture is inspired and so is never mistaken and never lies. The same cannot be said of interpreters.[21] Augustine interprets that Paul does not hide the truth when he writes that he saw what was going on, decided that he needed to say something to Peter publicly, and did so. Jerome chooses instead to find the truth in Scripture in what the apostles might have done, in order to explain away the embarrassing story that Paul publicly rebuked the more senior apostle.

---

19. Galatians 2:15–16.
20. Augustine, *Letters 1–99*, 75.8–11.
21. Augustine, *Letters 1–99*, 82.24.

The dispute about this episode in *Galatians* is not the only point of contention between the two scholars during their first exchange of letters. They also argue about whether the Hebrew Old Testament or the Septuagint is more authoritative for those who cannot read and understand Greek. Augustine asks Jerome to clarify the work of Origen and to make it more available through translation. More firmly related to their disagreement about *Galatians* are their differing expectations for Christian friendship, which seem to feed the vehemence of some moments in their exchange. Scholars have for some time now debated as to the cause, or causes, of their sometimes rancorous words.[22] Some have blamed Jerome's fiery nature; others Augustine's ambition,[23] tactlessness,[24] pomposity,[25] or even a tendency to bully.[26] Carriker protests, citing Grützmacher, who says that Augustine's "chivalry and modesty" saved the whole exchange from turning into a "bitter squabble."[27] Jennifer Ebbeler places the dispute within the context of another friendship that Jerome had very recently ended. She makes the case that "Jerome's objection was to Augustine's incorporation of rebuke and correction in an explicitly epistolary—as opposed to *viva voce*—friendship."[28] According to her, while Jerome would agree with Augustine that friends should be frank with each other, particularly when they are in the wrong, to do so within a letter simply breaks the rules set out

---

22. See O'Connell, "When Saintly Fathers," 344–345: "Ask scholars of either St. Jerome or St. Augustine what they think of the correspondence between these two and you are likely to get a number of responses . . . like some meticulously wrought miniature, the dossier of their letters presents one of the most revealing, dramatic, and exhilarating portraits I know of Augustine and Jerome: a portrait of two genuine, thoroughly outsize human beings, and a record of their friendship—always difficult, sometimes stormy; on the face of it improbable, but at bottom quite inevitable."

23. Ebbeler, *Disciplining Christians*, 146–47: both Peter Brown and James J. O'Donnell have this interpretation.

24. Bonner, *Life and Controversies*, 147–48.

25. Kelly, *Jerome*, although Carriker ("Augustine's Frankness," 128) notes that Kelly goes on to give a balanced view of the correspondence, admitting Jerome could be cantankerous.

26. O'Connell, "When Saintly Fathers."

27. Carriker, "Augustine's Frankness," 128. The reference she makes is to G. Grützmacher, *Hieronymus* (3 vols., Leipzig, 1901–1908), especially volume 3, 134ff. Carriker also notes that Grützmacher does not take into account that Augustine wanted to keep his discourse with Jerome civil, because he wanted "to determine answers to specific theological problems, because solving these problems brings men closer to God" (132).

28. Ebbeler, *Disciplining Christians*, 102.

in classical education.²⁹ Public rebuke between Christians, furthermore, can cause scandal; and Jerome is none too pleased that Augustine's letter asking him to sing a *palinode* (a song of retraction, as will be discussed momentarily) has been published in Rome and elsewhere (although this was without Augustine's command or knowledge).³⁰ This motif of breaking the old rules on the side of Jerome, and enabling the transformation of all old laws, according to Augustine, runs consistently through the letters; and it harkens back to the initial dispute between Peter and Paul.

Concentrating more on the differing senses of selfhood that bear upon friendships, Kathleen Jamieson elaborates how this particular quarrel can be better understood when seen in light of Jerome's foregoing dispute with Rufinus. Taking into account the shared framework of classical rhetoric that Augustine is so delighted to emphasise, Jamieson traces Augustine's reference to the "Stesichoran palinode" through to what could have been its bitter end.³¹ The *palinode* in question refers to an incident that Isocrates relates, that Stesichorus mocked Helen of Troy, who then blinded him. As soon as he retracted his words in a *palinode*, he regained his sight.³² Little does Augustine know that when he demands this song of retraction, he is using the same classical reference that Jerome had employed toward Rufinus—with whom he had acrimoniously and very publicly fallen out. Augustine initially downplays the inference that Jerome has been blinded, but this is not enough. In Jamieson's analysis, "Augustine unwittingly had scraped off what little scar tissue had formed on an old, deep wound and, at the same time, had evoked Jerome's fear that a piece of painful personal history was about to repeat itself."³³ Jamieson argues convincingly that Jerome attributes all of his own previous motivations for using such a reference toward a friend turned enemy. The outcome of the feud between Jerome and Rufinus can be gleaned from Jerome's summary of the affair: "it is simpler

---

29. Ebbeler's argument sits within her larger thesis that "In Augustine's hands" the textual exchanges that those in the ancient world used in their "cultivation of *amicitia*" offered "the medium for the *in absentia* correction of supposedly errant Christians." She makes the case that: what was innovative about Augustine's epistolary practice was not his inclusion of rebuke in a letter . . . Instead it was his expectation that a letter or rebuke would be reciprocated, that it would initiate an ongoing correspondence between Augustine and the object of his epistolary correction." Ebbeler, *Disciplining Christians*, 7.

30. See Augustine, *Letters 1–99*, 40, 72, and 73.

31. Jamieson, "Stesichoran Palinode."

32. See Augustine, *Letters 1–99*, 151n5 and 260n5.

33. Jamieson, "Stesichoran Palinode," 362.

to protect oneself from a proclaimed enemy than from an enemy cloaked as a friend."[34] Upon Rufinus's death, Jerome continued to call the friend become enemy a snake and a scorpion.[35] Jamieson argues that the earlier failed intimate friendship—where a friend had turned into an enemy—is precisely the context in which to understand Jerome's conflict with the African father. She analyzes how it takes all of Augustine's gracious diplomacy to soothe some of the pain he has unwittingly caused. It will, though, never be possible for him to have a full friendship with Jerome.

The first set of letters between these church fathers spans from A.D. 394/5 to 405. In that significant period of time, Augustine was able to bring Jerome to the point of asking that they no longer send each other letters with questions but instead with words of love.[36] One might think that this would be enough, but Augustine would rather go further, into a deeper space of closeness in discourse between friends. Instead of arguing with each other, Jerome offers: "If you want, let us playfully exercise on the field of scriptures without causing injury to each other."[37] The disappointment in Augustine's response is palpable. When Augustine asks Jerome questions, he is not motivated by the desire to frolic in a grassy field. He is begging for help. Jerome might feel when studying Scripture that he is in a playground. Augustine, is, in his own words, somewhere very different: "like someone gasping for air in the mountains."[38] Taking stock of the situation, Augustine wonders on the page whether they have differing views of the roles of those who interpret Scripture. Scripture, says Augustine, is always true; but interpreters of Scripture can err. In charity, scholars need to point out where mistakes might have been made. Jerome forces him to see that not all Christian scholars agree on this point. The translator in Bethlehem does not think that a friendship can occur where one friend complains about something in the other. In contrast, Augustine thinks without this kind of openness there can be no friendship at all; for the very space of freedom in which *caritas* thrives is thereby being denied. Language between the two is telling. Jerome sets up barricades where Augustine thinks they have no

---

34. Jamieson, "Stesichoran Palinode," 361.
35. Jamieson, "Stesichoran Palinode," 361.
36. Augustine, *Letters 1–99*, 81.
37. Augustine, *Letters 1–99*, 81.
38. Augustine, *Letters 1–99*, 82.2.

place. The former, he argues, wants what is essentially a lesser love. Augustine desires something greater.[39]

Spaces of Freedom or of Tyranny: Companions in the Cosmopolis and the Ghetto

Throughout their letters, each of these scholars uses imagery to define the dimensions of scholarly Christian friendship. In so doing, they delineate their respective understandings of the range (restrictive or expansive) that Christian friendship can take. Before reviewing some of the key details in this respect, it is illuminating to recall Desmond's distinction in *The Intimate Universal*. There, he says, "we can take cosmopolis and ghetto as emblematic of two fundamental orientations to the universal and the intimate."[40] That is, the cosmopolis has to do with the extensive: it reaches out beyond, to communicate itself. In comparison, the ghetto is more intensive and particular, dependent upon inner, intimate resources that render the contours of our distinctive humanity.[41] It might seem that there is an intractable dissimilarity or conflict between the two, indicating that members of a cosmopolis can never bring to bear anything more intimate; and that those in the ghetto cannot reach beyond themselves, to transmit their interior awareness. Desmond proposes instead that cosmopolis and ghetto can work together, and that this cooperation is characteristic of a religious way of being in the world.[42] He contends that metaxological philosophers are alert to the possibilities for relationship, rather than dichotomy, between ghetto and cosmopolis—which is to say between particular and universal, private and public. Such attunement can overcome modern oppositions and at the same time foster human enrichment within the political arena.

Again, Augustine and Jerome would agree on the need for mutual recognition and help between Christians. They consider that Christian life demands an active life of virtue, which has implications for Christian communities on pilgrimage to the heavenly Jerusalem. Each, though, conveys a differing experience of what it means to live in Christian community. A few examples in their letters helps to make this point, and at the same

---

39. Augustine, *Letters 1–99*, 82.36.
40. Desmond, *Intimate Universal*, 23.
41. Desmond, *Intimate Universal*, 23.
42. Desmond, *Intimate Universal*, 11, 29.

time furthers the work of situating them in the cosmopolis, the ghetto, or somewhere between.

From his first letter to Jerome, it seems that Augustine assumes that he can depend upon a certain concord between them. He speaks of their "communion in the spirit"[43] and identifies with Jerome as a fellow pilgrim who, all the way from Bethlehem provides provisions for those on a common journey. In addition, Augustine claims to speak on behalf of the "whole zealous society of African churches," who would indubitably benefit from Jerome's wisdom.[44] In his next letter, Augustine describes himself as someone who "worries over the affairs of others and worldly ones at that."[45] More than anything, he wants to close the distance between himself and Jerome, to make a space for intimate friendship. He apologizes for writing a long letter (71),[46] with the excuse that he has felt, when writing, as if he were conversing with Jerome in person.[47] In letter 73 he exclaims: "See what the lands and seas that physically separate us do";[48] and later he refers to "our mutual desire" for friendship, which "hangs in the air without reaching its goal."[49]

Tellingly, while throughout the letters Jerome emphasises what happens when friends betray one another, Augustine concentrates on the joys of friendship. Grieving on behalf of Jerome for the loss of a friendship with Rufinus, Augustine describes himself as someone who can feel a sense of abandonment with his most intimate friends. When the whole world seems to be against him, he can rest in their companionship. This love between him and his friends, he says, is there because of their common love of God. He expresses:

> when I perceive that a man is aflame with Christian love and has become my loyal friend with that love, whatever of my plans and thoughts I entrust to him I do not entrust to a human being, but to him in whom he remains so that he is such a person. For God

---

43. Augustine, *Letters 1–99*, 28.1.1.
44. Augustine, *Letters 1–99*, 28.2.2
45. Augustine, *Letters 1–99*, 29.
46. This is the letter that accompanied copies of the two previous letters, in which he tries to explain what is essentially both a disagreement and a miscommunication.
47. Augustine, *Letters 1–99*, 71.
48. Augustine, *Letters 1–99*, 73.7.
49. Augustine, *Letters 1–99*, 73.8.

is love, and he who remains in love remains in God, and God in him (1 Jn 4:16)[50]

Augustine establishes an ontological and theological framework for the experience that he has of being with friends in true concord. Empathising with the wounded Jerome, he reflects that when one has experienced such love, one's sense of betrayal is the more intense when such a friend becomes an enemy. In all of Augustine's language concerning friendship, he emphasises the possibilities for *caritas*, or *agape*; these include the need for frank discussion, and for forgiveness when such frankness goes awry.

Jerome's responses, on the other hand, emphasise his preference to consider himself removed from larger society, and able to select only a few friends who do not challenge him. This explains why he prefers to be surrounded by protective friends, rather than to embark upon new exchanges with seeming friends who may in fact be enemies. Jerome proves increasingly concerned to contrast his monastic life with Augustine's role as a bishop. He characterises he and his fellow monks: "We who dwell in the monastery are buffeted by waves from this side and that, and have endured the trouble of our earthly pilgrimage."[51] He describes himself as "an old man hiding in his cell,"[52] but at the same time threatens that he has skill and the energy to come out to fight when necessary. Contrasting his life with that of Augustine, he emphasises: "it is not proper that I, who have sweated with toil in the monastery with my holy brothers from youth to this age, should dare to write something against a bishop of my communion..."[53] Of course, this does not stop him from criticizing the upstart African.[54] Later, he refers to Augustine as "a bishop renowned in the whole world," while Jerome is in his "small cell with the monks, that is, [his] fellow sinners."[55] And yet again, he enjoins Augustine to "teach the peoples and enrich the houses of Rome with the new harvest from Africa," while Jerome is content to "whisper in a corner of the monastery with a poor fellow who listens and

---

50. Augustine, *Letters 1–99*, 73.10.
51. Augustine, *Letters 1–99*, 39.2,2.
52. Augustine, *Letters 1–99*, 72.2,3.
53. Augustine, *Letters 1–99*, 72.4.
54. O'Connell discusses just how inconsistent Jerome is throughout his letters. At one moment he offers love, and then he wants to fight; at another he is too weak to take up arms, at another he claims he can beat Augustine to a pulp. O'Connell, "When Saintly Fathers," 348–49.
55. Augustine, *Letters 1–99*, 75.5.

reads."⁵⁶ Jerome later identifies Augustine with a crowd, which the bishop can "stir up" due to the reverence they have for him as a bishop. In contrast, such crowds would consider Jerome "almost decrepit, a man who pursues the privacy of the monastery and the countryside."⁵⁷

Further, Jerome is at pains to identify himself with small bands of friends or scholars who form with him a force with which to be reckoned. To paraphrase, Jerome writes to Augustine: some of "my close friends and vessels of Christ"⁵⁸ here in Jerusalem, where there are many good people, have warned me against people like you: you are out for the glory of winning an argument with an older scholar. Go back to your flatterers there in Hippo—I am sure you have plenty!⁵⁹ Earlier, Jerome threatens that he can be like Entellus, the boxer who looks old and weak in the *Aeneid*, but who can pommel the younger Dares to a pulp.⁶⁰ He warns immediately afterward of an old proverb: "The tired ox puts his foot down with more force."⁶¹ Military images pile up too, to call up the image of a warrior ready for battle with Augustine's honey-covered sword. He is an old veteran who has strength for and knows the skills of war; he can rise to the occasion when necessary. With him in his fortress are those who are willing to defend him; not traitors who question him on any particulars of scholarship—whether in translation or interpretation.

Augustine's responses to all this are firm, but at the same time placatory. He describes feeling, when reading Jerome's first threatening letter, like he was being comforted at one moment, and then slapped in the face at the next.⁶² Allusions to the need for a Christian to turn the other cheek when under attack are impossible to ignore. Insisting that he does not want to be offended, but wants instead to persist so that they can become friends, Augustine from this point on works to transform Jerome's rhetoric. Wounds inflicted by a friend, he argues, can be an act of love—for a true friend causes pain only in order to bring about proper health. This is the center of

---

56. Augustine, *Letters 1–99*, 75.7.22.
57. Augustine, *Letters 1–99*, 75.18.
58. Augustine, *Letters 1–99*, 72.1.2.
59. For a full discussion of the significance of the distinctions between frankness and flattery in the ancient world, morally, socially, and politically, see Konstan, "Friendship, Frankness and Flattery."
60. Augustine, *Letters 1–99*, 68.2.
61. Augustine, *Letters 1–99*, 68.2.
62. Augustine, *Letters 1–99*, 73.1.1.

Augustine's argument concerning intimacy between friends: where there is confidence in friendship, there can be true growth. When a friend in Christ inflicts such a critical wound, he is a doctor, not an enemy soldier. The honeyed sword to which Jerome referred earlier mixed metaphors of battle and of healing—the Epicureans would dip medicinal cups in honey to make the bitter remedy easier to take; Augustine chooses to ignore the rattling saber, both offering and accepting his medicine instead.

The contrasting imagery used throughout these letters indicates two different modes of community—each claiming to be agapeic. On the one hand, Jerome has his non-critical friends, who will protect and fight with him to the end. At the same time, he chooses friends who are the scholars gone before him. He follows Origen and others, taking interpretations from them, rather than offering original points of view. On the other, Augustine retreats from battle to be with his friends, in a space of rest that nourishes him in all he needs to do. Such rest is not mere play, because he and his friends immerse themselves in questions, particularly to do with Scripture. They do so freely, unreservedly challenging each other when necessary. This, as he emphasises, is nothing like frolicking in the fields. He is up in the mountains with his fellow pilgrims, gasping for air and seeking help.[63] Augustine's invitation to the mountains is essentially an offer to go into the furthest reaches of the human heart, by moving upward toward knowledge of God; he is offering to sojourn to the interior and the superior with Jerome. One hears Augustine's deflation as increasingly he realizes that he cannot share an intimate friendship with Jerome, certainly due to their lack of proximity but also to Jerome's reticence to take the risk that Augustine really does want to be a true friend. Augustine gradually discovers, in his letters with Jerome, significant limitations to the range of intimacy that Christian friends can sustain.

At the very least, Augustine's confidence that Christians acting in good faith and with similar passions in life can expect the intimacy of concord—even when separated from one another in space and time—is weakened. Nonetheless, all is not lost. Years later, Jerome writes to Augustine as though to a best friend. Tellingly, Jerome's imagery is still that of a warrior. In the battle against the Pelagians, he and Augustine have been on the same side; and Augustine has fought well.[64] He and Augustine carry

63. For a full discussion of the importance of the idea of ascent for Augustine, see for instance McLarney, *Psalms of Ascent*.

64. Augustine, *Letters 156–210*, 95: "You are famous throughout the world. Catholics

out polite and encouraging exchanges until Jerome dies in 419. If Augustine received at least some recompense in his strange battle with Jerome, metaxological thinkers can glean something too: a series of reflections on the possible dynamics of agapeic communities in political society, as well as some guidelines for maintaining Christian friendships while disputing.

At stake in this debate between Augustine and Jerome is, again, the relationship between cosmopolis and ghetto. Jerome's interpretation relies on the development of a theory of private teaching, such that he can—with others before him—read into the text what is not there: Peter and Paul plotting together a piece of theatre. Augustine begs Jerome: if this is really so, then tell me, please, how the reader is to know which parts of Scripture are to be taken at face value, and which need to be reinterpreted?[65] During the years of their exchanges, Augustine is working out his own theory of interpretation of Scripture, which would always emphasise the need to take for granted that Scripture speaks about what is literally true. Essentially, both the relationship between us and God, and between each other, is at stake. For, if what the inspired word of God says to us is a lie (even a useful one), then God is lying. If the only way that we can find the truth is through a special reading of what is before us, then we may as well be Manichaeans, or some other form of gnostic, with only a few knowing the secret message behind the words we see before us.

There is an even more substantial point at stake here: the study of Scripture can and does happen best when its foundations of divine love are recognized. This is at once a metaphysical principle, a hermeneutic key, and a political precept. Augustine's *City of God* makes the case that the most important citizenship does not rely on social status, or even on location. Those who possess a properly ordered love of God and cosmos can consider themselves citizens anywhere, in any time and place. Such citizens partake, then, of a kind of cosmopolitanism, whereby they are united with a community that spans both earth and heaven. Such cosmopolitan ideas are also embedded within his work *Teaching Christianity*, where one finds that the knowledge that Christ gives, through world, community of the saints, and Scripture, is not the province only of scholars. In principle, that is, knowledge of Christ is for all, though not all may come to know

---

revere and embrace you as the second founder of the ancient faith. And, what is a sign of greater glory, all the heretics despise you, and they persecute me with like hatred in order to slay with their desire those whom they cannot slay with swords."

65. See, for instance, Augustine, *Letters 1-99*, 40.3.3.

of or accept it. Before presenting his principles of hermeneutics—his key principles for how to read Scripture, and some important points for how to preach or convey the word of God to others—Augustine writes about how God speaks to us through his world. Creation, Augustine says, is filled with signs, pointing us to the Creator. In a key passage, he compares our wayfaring through the world as a pilgrimage, where we constantly have our destination in mind.[66] Whether the pilgrimage be local or cosmic, Christians know that the bonds formed between fellow travellers toward the heavenly goal are significant.

Those affiliations are impossible without a shared sense of purpose, defined according to *caritas*. So, it is entirely fitting that before writing about how to read, speak, and listen, he discusses what it means to love.[67] Love, he argues, is to be offered to each person that one meets:

> All people are to be loved equally; but since you cannot be of service to everyone, you have to take greater care of those who are more closely joined to you by a turn, so to say, of fortune's wheel, whether by occasion of place or time, or any other such circumstances.[68]

He goes on to explain that every person that one meets, including one's enemy, is, in a certain respect, to be loved like every other person. This is a love by which "we want . . . all . . . to love God together with us, and all our helping them or being helped by them is to be referred to that one single end."[69] The Augustinian cosmopolis is open to all who are capable of *caritas*, and that means every human person. Love comes first, and it makes way for all kinds of communications, as well as for an understanding of God's words to his people through Scripture.

Augustine rejects what he sees as the false hierarchy that would say that only a few know what Scripture literally says. Instead, he strives to form intimate communities with Christians, so that they can delve together into the deeper (and at the same time higher) meanings of God's word. He invites Jerome to join him, and expresses what is needed for such a community to work. Augustine argues that intimate friends of this kind

---

66. Augustine, *Teaching Christianity*, 1.3.3—4.4.

67. For a discussion of Augustine's insistence that conferral between friends, often in unspoken form, is crucial before true confession can happen, see Vessey, "Conference and Confession."

68. Augustine, *Teaching Christianity*, 1.28.29.

69. Augustine, *Teaching Christianity*, 1.29.30.

need to be frank with one another, so that open rebuke becomes a sign of true friendship alongside expressions of admiration and delight in shared concerns and passions. His letters to Jerome contain an implicit set of rules, or prerequisites, for carrying out a genuine exchange that will bring each potential friend into a deeper Christian experience of community. Mark Vessey argues that friendship becomes increasingly important as the basis for which proper interpretation can take place, with *Teaching Christianity* and *Confessions* dependent upon "a text act performed jointly by two or more human beings in the presence of God and in the spirit of charity."[70] The results of such a conference, or *conlatio*, were then made public, to benefit all. In his letters to Jerome, Augustine brings to the fore that humans can err when they interpret; and his idea of such conference includes his insistence that friends correct each other when necessary.

It does seem that he and Jerome think differently about the role of friendship for that important act of interpretation of Scripture. In this wise, a distinction between two different modes of asceticism in the early church can be helpful. Douglas Robinson identifies Jerome as an eremitic and Augustine cenobitic.[71] Eremitic asceticism tends to favour the lone scholar, who brings the particularity and fire of his own life into the way that he translates. The cenobitic translator is, in contrast, calm and driven toward more objectivity of analysis.[72] The latter may not be attributes that we usually ascribe to Augustine, whose personality seems to emerge through everything that he writes.[73] However, this distinction brings to light again the way that Augustine approaches God, self, others, and the world of signs that includes Scripture. What he finds to be true of himself is tested in community with others, and ultimately in the community of being. To an important extent, it matters not who is carrying out a certain interpretation, and why: if it is wrong, it must be thwarted. Jerome can and does list as many scholars as he likes who agree with him; Augustine is unmoved, for the onus of proof is in how well an interpretation furthers both knowledge and loving engagement with divine love.

---

70. Vessey, "Conference and Confession."

71. Robinson, "Ascetic Foundations." For more on the ascetic tradition, see Rousseau, *Ascetics, Authority*, especially "Part Three: Jerome," 99–142.

72. Robinson, "Ascetic Foundations," 7.

73. Turner, *Thomas Aquinas*, 4.

Rules for Friendship: Inflicting and Healing Wounds

Augustine finds the basis for interpretation of Scripture in the experience of intimate friendship. Intimate exchanges between Christians become the occasion for God's love to inspire true interpretation of his word. Investigating what this agapeic communal mode of exploration looks like in practice, one finds three main rules in the letters from Augustine to Jerome. Firstly, intimate friends are to be frank with each other. Secondly—and dependent on the first point—theirs is to be a proper exchange, particularly in that each friend is expected to carry out a critique of the other's work, so that through the sweet disagreements that Augustine already experienced earlier in his life, together they can come closer to the truth.[74] Finally, when a Christian (particularly a Christian scholar) has made an error, it is his or her duty to retract that error, in public where necessary, to prevent more harm to others. At the same time, the retractor needs to accept, and even forgive, the one who has pointed out where he has lost his way. Indeed, Augustine goes so far as to quote Cicero, who maintains that an enemy who rebukes is better for the soul than a friend who is afraid to do so.[75] For friends to meet the demands of *caritas*, they must enter a space that demands a certain finesse. This is no field of flowers; nor, however, is it a war front. Augustine thinks that it is important to inflict a wound with the purpose of healing, when the need arises. This is precisely where Jerome disagrees.

Augustine's domain of friendship, that is, demands the virtue of frankness as a form of medicine. Frankness is to be employed as much for the self toward the self as the self toward the other. Entreating Jerome to be a good friend to himself, Augustine says: "... take up, I implore you, a frank and truly Christian severity combined with love in order to correct and amend your work..."[76] Augustine's claim that frankness, even to the point of reproach, demonstrates a greater love than flattery, has its precedents in Greek (particularly Athenian) and Roman thought.[77] While Augustine sometimes uses the term *libertas* or a derivative when referring to frankness in other letters, here he takes the word that Cicero employs in his writings,

---

74. See, for instance, Augustine, *Confessions*, 4.8.13.

75. Augustine, *Letters 1–99*, 73.4.

76. This is Carriker's translation, as found in Carriker, "Augustine's Frankness," 124.

77. Termed *parrhesia* by the Greeks, it was later translated in the days of the Roman republic and early empire as *libertas* or *licentia*; while in the biblical texts of the Septuagint it becomes *fiducia, fidentia,* or *constantia*, emphasizing that the origins of frankness are in a relationship of trust with God. See Konstan, "Friendship, Frankness and Flattery."

when the ancient statesman refers to someone of free birth, and also to a person upright and frank.[78] Thus the term that Augustine chooses has a salient link to freedom in the moral life as well as in public discourse and activity. The implication might be drawn that someone who can be frank between friends can offer the same virtue in more public forums.

Such freedom to speak is essential both to the intimacy proper to friendship and to the functioning of a greater cosmopolis. This relates to a problem that has already been indicated, which is that Augustine takes seriously both that one can have a group of intimate friends, and at the same time that *caritas* is to be extended to every person. So, while there is a qualitative difference between my intimate friends and others, at the same time I must love everyone equally—and as I love myself. For Augustine, an intimate friend is another self in a very particular way; and yet at a universal level, I am to love all others as I do myself. In such a view, Christian love seems insuperably demanding, and enacting the duties of love fraught with difficulty. To make the matter more complex, Augustine finds with Jerome that even though he might share the Christian faith, similar life experience, and interests with another person, this does not mean that the other will consider him a friend. The other will necessarily have confidence in, or trust, the aspiring friend.

Again, these problems can be approached by considering themes that again arise within Desmond's analysis of the possibilities and pitfalls of friendship. In *The Intimate Universal*, Desmond discusses "agapeics" and how every form of friendship is grounded in the intimacy of being. Namely, we both receive (*passio essendi*) and proffer (*conatus essendi*) the possibilities of relationships with others, and in those associations, we are attuned to the "happenings" of being.[79] Friendship, according to Desmond's analysis, can foster the conditions that counteract a human tendency toward tyranny—where a desire to overcome the other surpasses all other capacities. This is *eros turannos*, about which the ancients warn us, and Desmond asks whether friendships might even be enough to "save"[80] us from the wretchedness that pervades modern societies of isolation. The possibilities

---

78. Simpson, *Cassell's Latin Dictionary*, s.v. "ingenue," "ingenuitas," "ingenuus." Augustine also paraphrases Cicero, who writes in *De amicitia* that "enemies who rebuke us are generally more beneficial than friends who are afraid to rebuke us" (*De am* 24.90; Augustine, *Letters 1-99*, 72.4).

79. Desmond, *Intimate Universal*, 402–3.

80. Desmond, *Intimate Universal*, 366.

for such salvation through *philia* can be known through the "gifts"[81] that friendship brings. Friends come to us with and through being, and point to the community that is at the heart of the cosmos. In other words, the desire that Jerome occasionally shows, to subdue the other to his will and to emerge victorious, could be ameliorated through true friendship. Augustine's imagery of healing can be better appreciated in light of Desmond's analysis of the true source of human friendship and communication.

Augustine's experience with Jerome indicates that each person involved in a potential friendship needs to be alive to the subtle forms that it is appropriate for a Christian relationship to take. This requires its own modes of *finesse*, such that friends can together find how being presents itself to us as a community. The modes through which friendship operates, then, become increasingly fulfilling, the more friends enter into what Desmond terms "the agapeics of the intimate universal."[82] This is the space in which friends can have confidence in each other,[83] achieve a sense of balance in reciprocity,[84] enjoy one another's company,[85] be able to forgive one another,[86] and ultimately be companioned in being.[87] The notion of a companion relies on the potencies within being. Explicitly, the hospitality of being is the foundation for all such forms of being together; ultimately in agapeic community. Clearly, metaxological philosophy entails that companionship sheds light on being itself. Friendship is no mere addition to the cosmos: its demands are metaphysical.

Effectively, Augustine and Jerome fall short of meeting such demands. Augustine's analysis of why this is the case is illuminative. He will accept a lesser friendship with Jerome, but first he addresses the obstacles to what could have been a fuller, more exhilarating friendship.[88] Namely, Augustine has come across as impetuous and boastful; his questions have been too childish in Jerome's eyes; his language has been too harsh. Speaking candidly, Augustine observes all the same that had Jerome been willing to let him speak freely, without attributing motivations other than love to his

---

81. Desmond, *Intimate Universal*, 370.
82. See the title of chapter 8 in Desmond, *Intimate Universal*.
83. Desmond, *Intimate Universal*, 370.
84. Desmond, *Intimate Universal*, 379–81.
85. Desmond, *Intimate Universal*, 377.
86. Desmond, *Intimate Universal*, 392.
87. Desmond, *Intimate Universal*, 403.
88. See Augustine, *Letters 1–99*, 82.

words, matters might have proceeded differently. You only want me to approve of everything you say, says Augustine; when I do not do that, you become angry. Under such conditions, there is no freedom, and there can be no free play of friendship. What Desmond refers to as the precondition of confidence, is quite simply missing.[89]

A connection, finally, can be made between the confidence that Augustine longs for, and the importance of vulnerability in friendship, which Desmond discusses when analyzing the sources for enmity. Friends, Desmond argues, create between them a space of both the *passio essendi* and the *conatus essendi*, where a delicate balance needs to be struck.[90] This is a realm of risk, where each comes to know the other intimately, and this knowledge can double back on itself, either in love or in hatred. The energies that arise between friends indicate the "potentially limitless vulnerability of the human being," he argues.[91] At the end of this piece, Desmond observes that sometimes the only resource one has toward an enemy, is simply to let them be.

Desmond observes that simply to offer one's enemy such freedom is a kind of forgiveness. This brings us to the boundary of ethics that he speaks of elsewhere in *Philosophy and Its Others*—where we discover the threshold between ethics and religion.[92] Augustine finally does let Jerome be—but as a friend rather than an enemy, and stopping short of what he had desired. For, Augustine has never considered Jerome his enemy; refusing to be cast in this light, he has instead increasingly insisted that he offers Jerome only love—and the rarest form of love at that. He is willing to be the victim of Jerome's threats, repeatedly. Repetitively, he offers his other cheek. Jerome certainly gives him every opportunity to run away. Bloodied but not beaten, Augustine stands up again in the ring. Dares rises to the occasion, and Entellus finally sighs and gives in—but only after again dictating his own terms.

In Augustine's final plea, a tinge of dejection sounds, at an opportunity lost. His friendship with Jerome can never achieve the depth of intimacy

---

89. See Burt, *Friendship and Society*, 66, for Augustine on the importance of trust in friendship.

90. Desmond, "Enemies," 296. See also Desmond, *Intimate Strangeness*, chapter 8: "The Confidence of Thought: Between Belief and Metaphysics," an essay that brings together the themes of confidence and companionship, and argues for companionship between religion and metaphysics.

91. Desmond, "Enemies," 296.

92. Desmond, *Philosophy and Its Others*, 201–4.

that he longs for with all of his friends in Christ. With them, he constantly hopes, he can depend upon the possibility of experiencing the richness of *agape* not only offered (owed to every person as neighbor) but reciprocated (possible only with friends in Christ). If fraternal love really is impossible between us, says Augustine to Jerome, then we will need to settle for something that at least is not wrong for the Christian. Jerome disallows mutual criticism in their exchanges, which falls short both of the example set by the early apostles, and the hopes of a cosmopolitan Christian community that expands in reach while maturing in richness. In Augustine's words, "... that love that I want to have with you is certainly greater, but this smaller love [that you offer] is something better than no love at all."[93] This "better than nothing" is still less than the absolving words "it is nothing" that Desmond speaks of elsewhere—the forgiving words that one friend can offer to another.[94] Augustine refers to what he and Jerome now have as *minor caritas*, and perhaps he hopes that this can grow into the *maior caritas* that citizens of the City of God should share with one another. In any case, neither now acts as though they are enemies.

The correspondence between Augustine and Jerome indicates that Christians can experience a form of universal companionship that has the characteristics of cosmopolitan friendship. Focusing on the universal, they can easily agree about what they share with all other Christians. To achieve this, they only need to have in common the sense of being companions on a journey who agree to steer clear of disagreement. Augustine's sense of loss and disappointment is grounded in the knowledge that *caritas* demands, and at the same time can offer, so much more than this. According to his universal *and* intimate aspirations, Christians can expect from their true friends relationships of intimacy where they can challenge each other in love. In this way, they are more hardy colleagues on that pilgrimage toward the heavenly Jerusalem. As one gasps for air, the other can offer the oxygen of steady companionship in God's love.

Perhaps, in the end, Augustine's conceptual fault is in assuming that human words can be interpreted with the *caritas* that Scripture properly demands. God's word can always be depended upon; it is the personal outpouring of divine love. Human words can never attain the same level. This makes sense of another theme that carries through the letters discussed here. Augustine proclaims that when he writes to Jerome, he feels as if

93. Augustine, *Letters 1–99*, 82.36.
94. Desmond, *God and the Between*, 287.

Jerome is with him. If this were actually the case, he writes from Hippo, all of their misunderstandings would be swiftly resolved. Face-to-face, living, spoken words would make a difference. Jerome accuses Augustine of wielding a honeyed sword—dipping criticism in flattery; the older father thinks of frank words as weapons. Augustine labors to convey, in response, that sharp words between Christians can be the instruments of healing. He partially succeeds. To adapt the metaphor that Jerome adopts: Augustine does not consider that he is wielding a honeyed sword on the battlefield; he is approaching a fellow Christian with medicine that should not need to be delivered with the honey of flattery.

It may, after all, be impossible in all situations to achieve companionship in the cosmopolis that bears the marks of intimacy usually associated with ghetto. Between Christians, this requires *caritas* so that virtues can be formed that incorporate a willingness to listen to another, receiving and extending poignant words of love. If, as Desmond points out, such potencies in community derive from the community of beings, then more is always possible. In an age where discussions between scholars are increasingly in writing, at a speed that militates against reflection on the demands of *caritas*, there is perhaps an even greater need to act with the virtues proper to friends on pilgrimage to the eternal city. These are only some of the demands for companions in the *metaxu*.

Bibliography

Adams, Jeremy D. "Augustine's Definitions of *Populus* and the Value of Civil Society." In *The City of God: A Collection of Critical Essays*, edited by Dorothy F. Donnelly, 171–82. New York: Peter Lang, 1995.

Arendt, Hannah. *Love and Saint Augustine*. Edited by Joanna Vecchiarelli Scott and Judith Chelius Stark. Chicago: University of Chicago Press, 1996.

Arnold, Morris LeRoy. *The Soliloquies of Shakespeare: A Study in Technic*. New York: Columbia University Press, 1911.

Augustine. *The Confessions*. Translated by Maria Boulding. The Works of Saint Augustine: A Translation for the 21st Century 1/1. Hyde Park, NY: New City, 1997.

———. *Confessions*. Translated by R. S. Pine-Coffin. Harmondsworth: Penguin, 1971.

———. *Confessions*. Translated by Rex Warner. New York: Penguin, 1984.

———. *The City of God* (*De Civitate Dei*). Volume 1: books 1–21. Translated by William Babcock. The Works of Saint Augustine: A Translation for the 21st Century 1/6. Hyde Park, NY: New City, 2012.

———. *The City of God* (*De Civitate Dei*). Volume 2: books 11–22. Translated by William Babcock. The Works of Saint Augustine: A Translation for the 21st Century 1/7. Hyde Park, NY: New City, 2013.

———. *The Excellence of Marriage* (*De Bono Conjugali*). In *Marriage and Virginity*, translated by Ray Kearney, 29–64. The Works of Saint Augustine: A Translation for the 21st Century 1/9. Hyde Park, NY: New City, 1999

———. *Expositions of the Psalms* (*Enarrationes in Psalmos*) *1–32*. Translated by Maria Boulding. The Works of Saint Augustine: A Translation for the 21st Century 3/15. Hyde Park, NY: New City, 2000.

———. *Expositions of the Psalms* (*Enarrationes in Psalmos*) *99–120*. Translated by Maria Boulding. The Works of Saint Augustine: A Translation for the 21st Century 3/19. Hyde Park, NY: New City, 1999.

———. *Letters* (*Epistulae*) *1–99*. Translated by Roland J. Teske. The Works of Saint Augustine: A Translation for the 21st Century 2/1. Hyde Park, NY: New City, 2001.

———. *Letters* (*Epistulae*) *100–155*. Translated by Roland J. Teske. The Works of Saint Augustine: A Translation for the 21st Century 2/2. Hyde Park, NY: New City, 2003.

———. *Letters* (*Epistulae*) *156–210*. Translated by Roland J. Teske. The Works of Saint Augustine: A Translation for the 21st Century 2/3. Hyde Park, NY: New City, 2004.

———. *The Literal Meaning of Genesis*. In *On Genesis*, translated by Edmund Hill, 155–506. The Works of Saint Augustine: A Translation for the 21st Century 1/13. Hyde Park, NY: New City, 2002.

BIBLIOGRAPHY

———. *Sermons 1–19*. Translated by Edmund Hill. The Works of Saint Augustine: A Translation for the 21st Century 3/1. Hyde Park, NY: New City, 1990.

———. *Sermons 51–94*. Translated by Edmund Hill. The Works of Saint Augustine: A Translation for the 21st Century 3/3. Hyde Park, NY: New City, 1991.

———. *Sermons 148–183*. Translated by Edmund Hill. The Works of Saint Augustine: A Translation for the 21st Century 3/5. Hyde Park, NY: New City, 1992.

———. *Soliloquies: Augustine's Inner Dialogue*. Translated by Kim Paffenroth. The Works of Saint Augustine: A Translation for the 21st Century. Hyde Park, NY: New City, 2000.

———. *Teaching Christianity (De Doctrina Christiana)*. Translated Edmund Hill. The Works of Saint Augustine: A Translation for the 21st Century 1/11. Hyde Park, NY: New City, 1996.

Boone, Mark J. *The Conversion and Therapy of Desire: Augustine's Theology of Desire in the Cassiciacum Dialogues*. Eugene OR: Pickwick, 2016.

Bonner, Gerald. *Saint Augustine of Hippo: Life and Controversies*. Norwich: Canterbury, 2002.

Brown, Lesley, ed. *The New Shorter Oxford English Dictionary: On Historical Principles*. Volume 2: N–Z. Oxford: Clarendon, 1973.

Burt, Donald X. *Friendship and Society: An Introduction to Augustine's Practical Philosophy*. Grand Rapids: Eerdmans, 1999.

———. "Friendship and Subordination in Earthly Societies." *Augustinian Studies* 11 (1991) 83–123.

Bury, R. G. *The Symposium of Plato*. Cambridge: W. Heffer, 1932.

Cain, Andrew. "'Vox Clamantis in Deserto': Rhetoric, Reproach, and the Forging of Ascetic Authority in Jerome's Letters from the Syrian Desert." *Journal of Theological Studies*, n.s., 57:2 (2006) 500–525.

Carriker, Anne P. "Augustine's Frankness in His Dispute with Jerome Over the Interpretation of Galations 2:11–14." In *Nova Doctrina Vetusque: Essays on Early Christianity in Honor of Fredric W. Schlatter, S.J.*, edited by Douglas Kries and Catherine Brown Tkacz, 121–38. New York: Peter Lang, 1999.

Chadwick, Henry. *Augustine*. Oxford: Oxford University Press, 1986.

———. *Augustine of Hippo: A Life*. Oxford: Oxford University Press, 2009.

Cicero. *On Friendship*. Translated by W. A. Falconer. Loeb Classic Library 154. Cambridge MA: Harvard University Press, 1923.

Clair, Joseph. *Discerning the Good in the Letters and Sermons of Augustine*. Oxford: Oxford University Press, 2016.

Cole-Turner, R. S. "Anti-Heretical issues and the Debate over Galations 2.11–14 in the Letters of Saint Augustine to Saint Jerome." *Augustinian Studies* 11 (1980) 155–66.

Collinge, William J. "Developments in Augustine's Theology of Christian Community Life after A.D. 395. *Augustinian Studies* 16 (1984) 49–63.

Colston, Ken. "*Macbeth* and the Tragedy of Sin." *Logos* 13:4 (2010) 60–95.

Conybeare, Catherine. "The City of Augustine: On the Interpretation of Civitas." In *Being Christian in Late Antiquity: A Festschrift for Gillian Clark*, edited by Carol Harrison et al., 138–55. Oxford: Oxford University Press, 2014.

Corrigan, Kevin, and Elena Glazov-Corrigan. *Plato's Dialectic at Play: Argument, Structure, and Myth in the Symposium*. University Park: Pennsylvania State University Press, 2005.

Bibliography

Dauphinais, Michael, Barry David, and Matthew Levering, eds. *Aquinas the Augustinian*. Washington, DC: Catholic University of America Press, 2007.

Delanty, Gerard. "The Cosmopolitan Imagination." *Revista CIDOB d'Afers Internacionals* 82/83 (September 2008) 217–30.

Derpmann, Simon. "Solidarity and Cosmopolitanism." *Ethical Theory and Moral Practice* 12:3 (2009) 303–15.

Desmond, William. "Analogy and the Fate of Reason." In *The Oxford Handbook of Catholic Theology*, edited by Lewis Ayres and Medi-Ann Volpe. Oxford Handbooks Online, 2016. doi: 10.1093/oxfordhb/9780199566273.013.4.

———. *Art, Origins, Otherness: Between Philosophy and Art*. Albany, NY: SUNY, 2003.

———. "Augustine's *Confessions*: On Desire, Conversion, and Reflection." *Irish Theological Quarterly* 47:1 (1980) 24–33.

———. *Being and the Between*. Albany, NY: SUNY, 1995.

———. *Beyond Hegel and Dialectic*. Albany, NY: SUNY, 1992.

———. *Desire, Dialectic, and Otherness*. New Haven, CT: Yale University Press, 1987.

———. *Ethics and the Between*. Albany, NY: SUNY Press, 2001.

———. "'Exceeding Virtue': Aquinas and the Beatitudes." In *Thomas Aquinas: Scholar, and Thinker*, edited by James McEvoy, Michael W. Dunne, and Julia Hynes, 28–49. Dublin: Four Courts, 2011.

———. *The Gift of Beauty and the Passion of Being: On the Threshold between the Aesthetic and the Religious*. Eugene, OR: Cascade, 2018.

———. *God and the Between*. Oxford: Blackwell, 2008.

———. *Hegel's God: A Counterfeit Double*. Aldershot: Ashgate, 2003.

———. "Hyperbolic Thoughts." In *Framing a Vision of the World: Essays in Philosophy, Science, and Religion*, edited by Santiago Sia and André Cloots, 23–43. Leuven: Leuven University Press, 1999.

———. *The Intimate Strangeness of Being: Metaphysics after Dialectic*. Washington, DC: Catholic University of America Press, 2012.

———. *The Intimate Universal: The Hidden Porosity among Religion, Art, Philosophy, and Politics*. New York: Columbia University Press, 2016.

———. "'It Is Nothing'—Wording the Release of Forgiveness." *Proceedings of the ACPA* 82 (2008) 1–23.

———. "Neither Servility nor Sovereignty: Between Metaphysics and Politics." In *Theology and the Political: The New Debate*, edited by Creston Davis, John Milbank, and Slavoj Zizek, 153–82. Durham, NC: Duke University Press, 2005.

———. *Perplexity and Ultimacy: Metaphysical Thoughts from the Middle*. Albany, NY: SUNY Press, 1995.

———. *Philosophy and Its Others: Ways of Being and Mind*. Albany, NY: SUNY Press, 1990.

———. "Pluralism, Truthfulness and the Patience of Being." In *Health and Human Flourishing: Religion, Medicine, and Moral Anthropology*, edited by Carol R. Taylor and Roberto Dell'Oro, 53–68. Washington, DC: Georgetown University Press, 2006.

———. "Sticky Evil." In *God, Literature and Process Thought*, edited by D. Middleton, 133–55. Aldershot: Ashgate, 2002.

———. "Superiority Beyond Interiority: Augustinian Thoughts on the Intimate Universal." *Indian Journal of Philosophy and Religion*, 2019 (forthcoming).

———. "Tyranny and the Recess of Friendship." In *Amor Amicitiae: On the Love That Is Friendship: Essays in Medieval Thought and Beyond in Honor of the Rev. Professor*

James McEvoy, edited by Thomas Kelly and Philipp Rosemann, 99–125. Leuven: Peeters, 2004.

Dover, Kenneth. "Introduction." In *Plato's Symposium*, translated and edited by Kenneth Dover. Cambridge: Cambridge University Press, 1980.

Driver, Steven D. "The Development of Jerome's Views on the Ascetic Life." *Recherches de Théologie et Philosophie Médiévales* 62 (1995) 44–70.

Ebbeler, Jennifer. *Disciplining Christians: Correction and Community in Augustine's Letters*. Oxford: Oxford University Press, 2012.

Fiedrowicz, Michael. "General Introduction." In *On Genesis*, edited by John E. Rotelle, 153–66. The Works of Saint Augustine: A Translation for the 21st Century 1/13. Hyde Park, NY: New City, 2002.

Foley, Michael P. "A Spectacle to the World: The Theatrical Meaning of St. Augustine's Soliloquies." *Journal of Early Christian Studies* 22:2 (2014) 243–60.

Fox, Robin Lane. "Augustine's *Soliloquies* and the Historian." In *Studia Patristica XLIII: Augustine and Other Latin Writers*, edited by F. Young et al., 173–89. Leuven: Peeters, 2003.

Garber, Marjorie. *Shakespeare After All*. New York: Anchor, 2004.

Gregory, Eric. *Politics and the Order of Love: An Augustinian Ethic of Democratic Citizenship*. Chicago: University of Chicago Press, 2008.

Griffiths, Paul. "Secularity and the *Saeculum*." In *Augustine's City of God: A Critical Guide*, edited by James Wetzel, 33–54. Cambridge: Cambridge University Press, 2012.

Hackett, B. "Augustine and Prayer: Theory and Practice." In *Second Annual Course on Augustinian Spirituality*, 191–210. Rome: Pontifical Biblical Institute Press, 1976.

Hand, Thomas A. *Saint Augustine on Prayer*. Dublin: Gill and Son, 1963.

Harrison, Carol. *Beauty and Revelation in the Thought of St. Augustine*. Oxford: Clarendon, 1992.

———. "Measure, Number and Weight in Saint Augustine's Aesthetics." *Augustinianum* 28:3 (1998) 591–602.

Heyking, John von. *Augustine and Politics as Longing in the World*. Columbia: University of Missouri Press, 2001.

———. "The Luminous Path of Friendship: Augustine's Account of Friendship and Political Order." In *Friendship and Politics: Essays in Political Thought*, edited by John von Heyking and Richard Avramenko, 115–38. Notre Dame, IN: University of Notre Dame Press, 2008.

Hirsch, James. "Shakespeare and the History of Soliloquies." *Modern Language Quarterly* 58:1 (1997) 1–26.

Hunter, Richard. *Plato's Symposium*. Oxford: Oxford University Press, 2004.

Jackson, M. G. St. A. "Faith, Hope and Charity and Prayer in St. Augustine." *Studia Patristica* 22 (1989) 265–70.

———. "The Lord's Prayer in St. Augustine." *Studia Patristica* 27 (1993) 312–21.

Jamieson, Kathleen. "Jerome, Augustine and the *Stesichoran Palinode*." *Rhetorica: A Journal of the History of Rhetoric* 5:4 (1987) 353–67.

Kierkegaard, Søren. "Speech in Praise of Abraham." In *Fear and Trembling*, translated by Alistair Hannay, 49–56. London: Penguin, 1995.

Konstan, David. "Friendship, Frankness and Flattery." In *Friendship, Flattery and Frankness of Speech: Studies on Friendship in the New Testament World*, edited by John Fitzgerald, 7–20. Leiden: Brill, 1996.

———. "Problems in the History of Christian Friendship." *Journal of Early Christian Studies* 4:1 (1996) 87–113.
Ladner, G. B. "Saint Augustine and the Difference between the Reform Ideas of the Christian East and West." In *The Idea of Reform: Its Impact on Christian Thought and Action in the Age of the Fathers*, 153–283. Cambridge, MA: Harvard University Press, 1959.
Lee, James K. "Babylon Becomes Jerusalem: The Transformation of the Two Cities in Augustine's *Enarrationes in Psalmos*." *Augustinian Studies* 47:2 (2016) 157–80.
Lubac, Henri de. "Patristic Origins: Saint Augustine?" In *The Four Senses of Scripture*, translated by Mark Sebane, 123–33. Medieval Exegesis 1. Edinburgh: Eerdmans, 1998.
Markus, Robert. *Saeculum: History and Society in the Theology of St. Augustine*. Cambridge: Cambridge University Press, 1970.
Maschke, Timothy. "St. Augustine's Theology of Prayer: Gracious Conformation." In *Collectanea Augustiniana: Augustine Presbyter Factus Sum*, edited by Joseph T. Lienhard et al., 431–46. New York: Peter Lang, 1993.
McLarney, Gerard. *St. Augustine's Interpretation of the Psalms of Ascent*. Washington, DC: Catholic University of America Press, 2014.
McGuirk, James. "Eros, Power and Justice: William Desmond and his Others." In *Between System and Poetics: William Desmond and Philosophy after Dialectic*, edited by Thomas Kelly, 163–74. Aldershot: Ashgate, 2007.
McNamara, M. A. *Friends and Friendship in Saint Augustine*. Staten Island, NY: Alba House, 1964.
———. *Friendship in Saint Augustine*. Fribourg: Fribourg University Press, 1958.
Moore, Duston. "Plurivocal Eros: A Metaxological Reading of Plato's *Symposium*. In *Between System and Poetics: William Desmond and Philosophy after Dialectic*, edited by Thomas Kelly, 163–74. Aldershot: Ashgate, 2007.
Nawar, Tamer. "Augustine on the Dangers of Friendship." *The Classical Quarterly* 65:2 (2015) 836–51.
Nicgorski, Walter. "Cicero's Distinctive Voice on Friendship: *De Amicitia* and *De Re Publica*." In *Friendship and Politics: Essays in Political Thought*, edited by John von Heyking and Richard Avramenko, 84–114. Notre Dame, IN: University of Notre Dame Press, 2008.
Nussbaum, Martha. *The Fragility of Goodness: Luck and Ethics in Greek Tragedy and Philosophy*. Rev. ed. Cambridge: Cambridge University Press, 2001.
O'Connell, Robert J. "When Saintly Fathers Feuded: The Correspondence between Augustine and Jerome." *Thought: A Review of Culture and Idea* 54 (1979) 344–64.
O'Donovan, Oliver. "Augustine's *City of God* XIX and Western Political Thought." In *The City of God: A Collection of Critical Essays*, edited by Dorothy F. Donnelly, 135–49. New York: Peter Lang, 1995.
Oort, Johannes van. *Jerusalem and Babylon: A Study into Augustine's City of God and the Sources of His Doctrine of the Two Cities*. New York: Brill, 1991.
Pickstock, Catherine. "What Shines Between: The *Metaxu* of Light." In *Between System and Poetics: William Desmond and Philosophy after Dialectic*, edited by Thomas Kelly, 107–22. Aldershot: Ashgate, 2007.
Pieper, Josef. *The Silence of Saint Thomas*. Translated by John Murray and Daniel O'Connor. Chicago: Henry Regney, 1957.

Plato. *Symposium*. Translated by Michael Joyce. In *The Collected Dialogues of Plato*, edited by Edith Hamilton and Huntington Cairns, 526–74. Princeton, NJ: Princeton University Press, 1961.

Robinson, Douglas. "The Ascetic Foundations of Western Translatology: Jerome and Augustine." *Translation and Literature* 1 (1992) 3–25.

Rousseau, Philip. *Ascetics, Authority, and the Church in the Age of Jerome and Cassian*. Oxford Historical Monographs. Oxford: Oxford University Press, 1978.

Sartre, Jean-Paul. *Existentialism Is a Humanism*. Translated by Carol Macomber. New Haven, CT: Yale University Press, 2007.

Scott, Gary Alan, and William A. Welton. *Erotic Wisdom: Philosophy and Intermediacy in Plato's Symposium*. Albany, NY: SUNY Press, 2008.

Shakespeare, William. *Macbeth*. Edited by Sandra Clark and Pamela Mason. The Arden Shakespeare. London: Bloomsbury, 2015.

Shapiro, James. *1606: William Shakespeare and the Year of Lear*. London: Faber, 2015.

Sheffield, Frisbee C. C. *Plato's Symposium: The Ethics of Desire*. Oxford: Oxford University Press, 2006.

Simpson, Christopher Ben. "All Things Shining: Desmond's Metaxological Metaphysics and *The Thin Red Line*." In *Between System and Poetics: William Desmond and Philosophy after Dialectic*, edited by Thomas Kelly, 239–59. Aldershot: Ashgate, 2007.

———. *Religion, Metaphysics, and the Postmodern: William Desmond and John D. Caputo*. Bloomington, IN: Indiana University Press, 2009.

Simpson, D. P. *Cassell's Latin Dictionary: Latin-English; English-Latin*. 26th ed. London: Cassell, 1952.

Skiffington, Lloyd A. *The History of English Soliloquy: Aeschylus to Shakespeare*. Lanham, MD: University Press of America, 1985.

Stock, Brian. *Augustine's Inner Dialogue: The Philosophical Soliloquy in Late Antiquity*. Cambridge: Cambridge University Press, 2010.

———. *The Integrated Self: Augustine, the Bible, and Ancient Thought*. Philadelphia: University of Pennsylvania Press, 2017.

———. "The Philosophical Soliloquy." In *The Integrated Self: Augustine, the Bible, and Ancient Thought*, 98–126. Philadelphia: University of Pennsylvania Press, 2017.

———. "Self, Soliloquy, and Spiritual Exercises in Augustine and Some Later Authors." *Journal of Religion* 91:1 (2011) 5–23.

Targoff, Ramie. "'Dirty' Amens: Devotion, Applause and Consent in *Richard III*." *Renaissance Drama* 31 (2002) 61–84.

Thomas Aquinas. *Summa Theologiae*. Translated by the Fathers of the English Dominican Province. 5 vols. New York: Cosimo Classics, 2007.

———. *Truth: The Disputed Questions on Truth*. Translated by Robert W. Mullitan. 3 vols. Chicago: Henry Regney, 1952.

Turner, Denys. *Thomas Aquinas: A Portrait*. New Haven, CT: Yale University Press, 2013.

Tutewiler, Corey. "On the Cause of Metaphysical Indeterminacy and the Origin of Being." In *William Desmond and Contemporary Theology*, edited by Christopher Ben Simpson and Brendan Thomas Sammon, 93–116. Notre Dame, IN: University of Notre Dame Press, 2017.

Vessey, Mark. "Conference and Confession: Literary Pragmatics in Augustine's '*Apologia Contra Hironymum*.'" *Journal of Early Christian Studies* 1:2 (1993) 175–213.

Weaver, Rebecca H. "Prayer." In *Augustine Through the Ages: An Encyclopedia*, edited by Allan D. Fitzgerald, 670–75. Grand Rapids: Eerdmans, 1999.

Williams, Rowan. "Politics and the Soul: A Reading of *The City of God*." *Milltown Studies* 19/20 (1987) 55–72.
Wetzel, James. "Introduction." In *Augustine's City of God: A Critical Guide*, edited by James Wetzel, 1–13. Cambridge: Cambridge University Press, 2012.
Woo, B. Hoon. "Pilgrim's Progress in Society: Augustine's Political Thought in *The City of God*." *Political Theology* 16:5 (2015) 421–41.

Index

A

"aesthetics of happening," 41–42, 70–71
agape, 102–3
   eros and, 51–52
   service based on, 114, 117–18
analogy, 77–78
Aquinas, Thomas. *See* Thomas Aquinas
arche, the. *See* origin of creation
Art, Origins and Otherness (Desmond), 43
atheism, 22
Aufhebung (sublation), xix
Augustine
   City of God, 102, 103–4, 135
   companions of, xvii
   confession by, 68–69
   Confessions, 5–6, 15–17, 25, 28, 68–70
   conversion of, 15–17
   Descartes and, 65
   Desmond and, xvi–xvii
   friendship in, 103–10, 120, 131–32
   on grace in creation, 15
   Jerome and, 127–28, 134–35, 140–42
   on love, 136
   masks in, 68–71
   metaxological approach of, xix
   peacemaking in, 133–34
   prayer in, 49–50, 52–56
   restlessness of, 4
   route of desire toward God of, xvi–xvii, xix, 4, 55–56, 91
   on scripture interpretation, 126–27, 129, 135, 136–37
   Soliloquies, 83–88
   Teaching Christianity, 135–36
autonomy, 40

B

Beatitudes, the, 79
being
   affirmation of, 39–40
   analogy of, 78
   God and, 74–75
   goodness and, 4, 9, 12, 24–25, 38–39
   ground of, 6–7, 17
   hyperboles of, 41–43
   idiocy of, xviii, 10
   lack of, 28–29
   meaning and, xvii–xviii, 4
   overdetermination of, 88
   plurivocity of, 61
   transcendence and, 6
Being and the Between (Desmond), 110
between, the, xvii
Beyond Hegel and Dialectic (Desmond), 64–67

C

caritas, 14n32, 51, 84, 85–86, 103, 136
   concordia and, 106–7
Christ, Incarnation of, 13

Index

Christians
    interactions between, 107–8, 120–21, 124–25, 142
    philoi and, 122
Cicero, 107–8
citizenship, 135
City of God (divine order), 101, 103–4
City of God (work by Augustine), 102, 103–4, 135
City of Man (political order), 101, 103–4
Clair, Joseph, 108–9
commons, the. *See* political order
communication limits, 142–43
communities
    of agapeic service, 117–18
    defined, 103
    of distracted desire, 114–15
    of erotic sovereignty, 116–17
    families, 112–13
    forms of, 110–11
    intimacy and, 116–18
    love and, 111
companionship, x–xi, xiii, xv, 102
    Christian, 142
companionship in thought
    for Augustine, 122–23
    for Desmond, xvi–xvii
    issues concerning, 123–24
    for Jerome, 123
    norms for, 121–22
conatus essendi, 43
    defined, 36
concordia, 102, 131–32
    caritas and, 106–7
Confessions (Augustine), 5–6, 15–17, 25, 28
    as mask, 68–70
confidence, 140–41
conscience, 83, 89–90
consumerism, 115
conversion, 87
    creation and, 11–14, 16–17, 30
cosmopolis, 125
    in cooperation with ghetto, 130
    norms within, 121, 135–36

creation
    attentiveness to, 25–26
    block notion of, 21–23
    conversion and, 11–14, 16–17, 30
    dynamism of, 26
    God and, 77, 78
    as mask, 71
    mechanistic model of, 21–23
    nature of, 20
    origin of, 3
    overdetermination of, 23–24
creatureliness, 73
criticism, 120, 132–33
cupiditas, 14n32, 51, 85

D

deception, 91–92
Descartes, René, 65
desire, 84
    distracted, 115
    the good and, 51n50
    prayer and, 52–56
Desire, Dialectic and Otherness (Desmond), 3, 4–5
Desmond, William
    Art, Origins and Otherness, 43
    Augustine and, xvi–xvii
    Being and the Between, 110
    Beyond Hegel and Dialectic, 64–67
    on companionship in thought, xvi
    on cosmopolis and ghetto, 125
    Desire, Dialectic and Otherness, 3, 4–5
    on elemental awareness, 27, 57
    on ethical norms, 8
    Ethics and the Between, 7, 111, 112–13
    "Exceeding Virtue," 79
    on God and freedom, 30
    God and the Between, 21–23, 26, 32, 35, 36, 41–42, 53, 57, 62–63, 74–75, 111
    Intimate Strangeness of Being, The, 72, 75, 111–12
    Intimate Universal, The, 115, 130, 139–40

Index

kinship in, 110–15
on loss and nothingness, 28–29
"Neither Servility nor Sovereignty," 111
on overdetermination, 24
on passion of knowing in Augustine, 65
on peace, 80
on porosity to divine in *Summa Theologiae*, 72
on speculative thought in Aquinas, 66
dialectic, xviii, 9–10
dialogue, 90
disposability, 115, 116
divine communication, 83
double mediation (doubling), 62, 68, 89
analogy and, 77
dualism, 4, 13

E

Ebbeler, Jennifer, 127
elemental, the
attentiveness to, 57
communications of, 38–39, 57
the divine and, 23–28
evil and, 31–32
forgiveness and, 32
ends, 9, 12, 17–18
equivocation, 89, 91
equivocity, xviii, 8, 88–89
dialogue and, 90
univocity and, 90–91, 93
vision and, 85
eros, 9, 37n5, 44–45, 47, 103
agape and, 51–52
See also communities, of erotic sovereignty
Eros, 45, 47
ethics
awareness of, 83, 89–90
friendship and, 109–10
norms of, 8
Ethics and the Between (Desmond), 7, 111, 112–13
evil, 28–29
deeds of, 88, 92–96
the elemental and, 31–32
forgiveness and, 31–32
God and, 29
goodness and, 22–23
"Exceeding Virtue" (Desmond), 79

F

faith, 85
families, 112–13
agapeic service and, 114
figures
God and, 75–76
persons as, 76
"Five Ways" of Thomas Aquinas, 74–76
flesh, 13
See also dualism
forgiveness, 87–88, 141
the elemental and, 32
evil and, 31–32
frankness, 138–39
freedom, x, 29–30
to speak, 138–39
friendship, 102, 106–7
aspirations in, 134
in Augustine, 103–10, 120
Christian, 107–8
in Cicero, 107–8
concessions within, 141–42
confidence within, 140–41
criticism and, 120
ethics and, 109–10
expansion of, 108–9
finessing of, 140
forgiveness within, 141
givenness and, 140
in Jerome, 120
love and, 106–8
otherness and, 106
rules for, 138
solace of, 131–32
tyranny and, 139
vulnerability within, 141
fulfilment, 9, 12, 17–18

G

ghetto, 125
  in cooperation with cosmopolis, 130
  norms within, 121
givenness, 70–71
  friendship and, 140
God
  analogy and, 77–78
  in Augustine, 65
  being and, 74–75
  communication from, 83
  in Descartes, 65
  the elemental and, 23–28
  evil and, 29
  figures and, 75–76
  self-knowledge and, 86–87
  in Thomas Aquinas, 67
  world and, 77, 78
God and the Between (Desmond), 21–23, 26, 32, 35, 36, 41–42, 53, 57, 62–63, 74–75, 111
Godlessness, 40
good, the, 111
  being and, 4, 9, 12, 24–25, 38–39
  desire and, 51n50
  evil and, 22–23
  ground of being and, 7
  overdetermination of, 17
  privation of, 29
grace, 15
grief, 10–11
ground of being, 17
  the good and, 7
  origin of creation and, 6–7

H

happiness, 54–55
  love and, 51
health
  reason and, 84
  vision and, 85, 86
Hegel, Georg, xviii, 66, 75
hope, 85
humility, 87
hyperboles, 10n21
  of being, 41–43

I

idiocy of being, xviii, 10
ignorance, learned, 56, 58
Incarnation of Christ, 13
infinitude, 4–5
insanity, 94, 95
inspiration, 42–43
interdependence, 91, 97
interiority, 103
intermediation, 62
  analogy and, 78
intimacy, 109
  community and, 116–18
  familial, 112–13
  political life and, 103
Intimate Strangeness of Being, The (Desmond), 72, 75, 111–12
Intimate Universal, The (Desmond), 115, 139–40

J

Jamieson, Kathleen, 128–29
Jerome
  Augustine and, 127–28, 134–35, 140–42
  criticism in, 132–33
  friendship in, 120
  Rufinus and, 123, 128–29
  on scripture interpretation, 126–27, 129, 137

K

Kant, Immanuel, 75
Kierkegaard, Søren, 63–64
  on thought, 66
kinship, 101, 102
  in Desmond, 110–15
  marriage and, 104–6
  political order and, 104–6

L

lack of being, 28–29
learned ignorance, 56, 58
Lee, James K., 102
Leibniz, Gottfried, 22
love, 14–15
  citizenship and, 135

Index

communities and, 111
friendship and, 106–8
happiness and, 51
prayer and, 50
reason and, 84
silence and, 69, 70

M

Macbeth (character), 92–96
Macbeth (play by Shakespeare), 82–83, 92–96
Macbeth, Lady (character), 92–94
Manichaeism, 13
marriage, 104–6
mask/s, 61–64
    in Augustine, 68–71
    creation as, 71
    functions of, 61, 62
    as metaxological mediation, 62–63
    the self and, 62–63
    senses of the notion, 62
    in Thomas Aquinas, 71–77
meaning
    being and, xvii–xviii, 4
    nothingness and, 31
mediation, metaxological, 62–63
metaxological philosophy, x, xvii
    alternatives to, xvii–xix
    nature of, xvi
metaxu, xvii
monologue, 93, 95
moral order, 93

N

"Neither Servility nor Sovereignty" (Desmond), 111
Nietzsche, Friedrich, 89
nihilism, 12
nothingness
    meaning and, 31
    ultimacy and, 67

O

oikeiosis, 108–9
openness to transcendence, 64–68
    See also porosity

origin of creation, 3, 4, 10, 15–16
otherness, 42, 62
    friendship and, 106
    the self and, 111–12, 117
    use of, 116
overdetermination, 90
    of being, 88
    of creation, 23–24
    of the good, 17

P

passio essendi, 8n18, 10–11, 43
    defined, 36
patience, 36
Paul and Peter, Saints, 125–26
peace, 79–80
peacemaking, 133–34
Penia (Poverty), 45–47
persona, 62, 63
persons, 63
    as figures, 76
philoi, 122
philosophy
    metaxological, x, xvi–xix
    modern, ix
    religion and, xix, 66, 67
    theology and, x–xi, 35, 36, 38, 39, 49, 59, 88
Pieper, Josef, 73
Plato
    cave allegory of, 7
    Symposium, the, 37, 44–49
plurivocity
    analogy and, 77–78
    of being, 61
political order, 115, 116
    interiority and, 103
    intimacy and, 103
    kinship and, 104–6
    See also City of Man (political order)
Poros (Resource), 45–47
porosity, xv, xvi, 18, 36–37, 45–47, 58–59
    images of, 38–44
power, 36, 92
    will to, 89

Index

prayer, 6, 18, 57–58
   in Augustine, 49–50, 52–56
   desire and, 52–56
   love and, 50
   self-knowledge and, 84
   thought and, x–xi, xix, 35, 36, 38, 39, 49, 59, 66, 67, 88
prosopon, 62

R
rationalism, 22, 40
reason, 83–84, 86, 96–97
   health and, 84
   love and, 84
redemption, 32
religion, xix, 66, 67
restlessness, 4
"return to zero," 56, 58
Rufinus, 123, 128–29

S
"Sabbath for thought," 79
Sartre, Jean-Paul, 22
scholarship rules, 138
secularism, 101
self, the, 40
   masks and, 62–63
   otherness and, 117
   See also selving
self-knowledge, 87, 95–97
   God and, 86–87, 97
   prayer and, 84
self-mediation, 62
self-reflection, 62, 82–83, 87–88
self-transcendence, 79
selving, xv, 13, 17, 43
   defined, 110
   otherness and, 111–12
Shakespeare, William
   Macbeth, 82–83, 92–96
silence, 73
   love and, 69, 70
   of thought, 79–80
   wisdom and, 67
Socrates, 44–49
   trance of, 48–49
Socratic questioning, 8–9

Soliloquies (Augustine), 83–88
soliloquy
   defined, 83
   monologue and, 93, 95
spirit, 13
   See also dualism
sublation, xix
Summa Theologiae (Thomas Aquinas), 72
Symposium, the (Plato), 37, 44–49

T
Teaching Christianity (Augustine), 135–36
tears, 11
theism, 22
theology and philosophy, x–xi, 35, 36, 38, 39, 49, 59, 88
Thomas Aquinas
   on analogy, 78
   character of, 72–73
   Fifth Way of, 75–76
   God in, 67
   masks in, 71–77
   silence of, 73
   Summa Theologiae, 72
   Third Way of, 74–75
   on thought, 66–67
thought
   prayer and, x–xi, xix, 35, 36, 38, 39, 49, 59, 66, 67, 88
   silence of, 79–80
tragedy, 97
transcendence, 14
   being and, 6
   elemental relationship to, 25–27
   openness to, 64–68
   See also God
Turner, Denys, 72–73
tyranny, 139

U
univocity, xvii–xviii, 7
   equivocity and, 90–91, 93
   positive sense of, 7n15
   tyrannical, 89
utility, 115

Index

V

vision
    equivocity and, 85
    health and, 85, 86
    transformation of, 13–14
vulnerability, 141

W

weeping, 11
wisdom, 67
Word, the, 17
world, the. *See* creation

You may be interested in:

Church and World
Eusebius's, Augustine's, and Yoder's Interpretations of the Constantinian Shift

By Simon P. Schmidt

The question of how the church is to exist 'in but not of the world' is a much contested current theological debate. To provide answers true to the context in which the Western church now finds itself, it is worth investigating how the question has been answered in the past. In determining what to do today, we must understand how we got here in the first place.

Church and World looks to the fourth century, at the beginning of which people were persecuted for being Christians, and persecuted for not being Christians by the end. The change during the century raised fundamental questions about the relationship between church and state and nature of good government, which are as pressing today as they have ever been. Simon P. Schmidt offers an academic investigation of how three paradigmatic theologians interpreted this so-called Constantinian shift: Eusebius of Caesarea (ca. 260-339), Augustine of Hippo (354-430), and John Howard Yoder (1927-1997). Surprising similarities between the theology of Eusebius and Yoder become apparent, along with the underlying theological structures of how to interpret what it looks like to be a community that follows Christ.

Simon P. Schmidt holds a Cand.theol. from the University of Copenhagen, Denmark, and an MTS degree from Duke Divinity School, USA. His critical work on the relationship between church and state earned him a gold medal for academic achievement, paradoxically – considering the contents of Church and World – awarded by Danish Queen Margrethe II of Denmark, head of the Lutheran Church of Denmark. He is currently employed at Lund University (Sweden).

Paperback ISBN: 9780227177259
PDF ISBN: 9780227907269

You may be interested in:

Desire, Dialectic, and Otherness
An Essay on Origins (2nd Edition)

By William Desmond

Many philosophers since Hegel have been disturbed by the thought that philosophy inevitably favours sameness over otherness or identity over difference. William Desmond here offers a constructive and positive approach to the problem of difference and otherness. He systematically explores the question of dialectic and otherness by analysing how human desire inevitably seeks immanent wholeness in a manner that opens it to irreducible otherness. In a wide-ranging yet unified discussion, Desmond tackles such issues as the nature of the self, the ambiguous restlessness and inherent power of being revealed by human desire, desire's relation to transcendence, its openness to otherness in agapeic good will and in relation to the sublime as an aesthetic infinitude.

Desire, Dialectic, and Otherness is a remarkable introduction to Desmond's metaxological philosophy. This second edition contains a substantial new preface and an afterword to each chapter in which Desmond reflects on the material from the standpoint of his current thinking.

William Desmond is Professor of Philosophy at Katholieke Universiteit Leuven as well as David Cook Visiting Chair in Philosophy at Villanova University.

Paperback ISBN: 9780227174647
PDF ISBN: 9780227902745